VEGETARIAN COOKING STEP BY STEP

LENA TRITTO

GRUB STREET · LONDON

This English language edition published in 2015 by
Grub Street
4 Rainham Close
London
SW11 6SS

Email: food@grubstreet.co.uk
Twitter: @grub_street
Facebook: Grub Street Publishing
Web: www.grubstreet.co.uk

ISBN 978-1-910690-03-1

Contents

You are what you eat

This saying has become a cliché, but nothing could be closer to the truth. Scientific research over the last few decades has focused on the role diet plays in the health of every individual.

We live in a part of the world where every day is a battle against obesity and the growing number of cardiovascular diseases which could be prevented to a large degree by choosing healthy food and healthy lifestyles. What is more, today we know that over 30% of cancers are related to poor diet.

Starting with the assumption that you really are what you eat, taking an active and responsible attitude towards the food you place on your table is the means you have to achieve good health and a longer life. You can choose what is best for you; and with a little effort at the start, you can then get used to looking after your health in a simple and enjoyable way with food that pleases both the eye and the palate.

The simple, step-by-step, easy to follow recipes presented here are only a small but valuable example of this. But never forget that some foods are able to protect specifically against disease; and that's a good thing to know!

Research has shown that following a Mediterranean-style diet can reduce the chance of developing conditions such as heart disease, type 2 diabetes, high blood pressure, obesity and even Alzheimer's disease, and in addition The World Health Organization (WHO) and the UK Government's Change4Life campaign recommend we eat five portions of fruit and vegetables a day. Today many people believe that following a vegetarian diet characterised by a high intake of vegetables, pulses, fruit and whole grains is the healthiest diet of all. Protein comes mostly from nuts and pulses, carbohydrate comes largely from vegetables and some whole grains – usually non-gluten grains – and fat comes from nuts, seeds and cold-pressed nut and seed oils.

It is important to eat a wide variety of vegetables whatever your diet. They are rich in fibre and nutrients and help to protect the cardiovascular system. Certain vegetables are particularly beneficial, such as onions and garlic, beetroot, broccoli, celery, cabbage, chicory, Chinese cabbage, courgettes, kale, cucumbers, carrots, spinach, leeks, broccoli, asparagus, lettuce, cauliflower, aubergine, garlic and peppers.

Raw vegetables and vegetable juices are especially valuable. Vegetable juices are an excellent source of vitamins and minerals and other phyto-nutrients that have been shown to combat disease. Because juices are raw, the vitamin C and other water-soluble vitamins and enzymes that would be largely lost in cooking are still intact.

Consumption of all fruit (including dried fruits, because they have had most of their moisture removed) should be fairly moderate, as fruit is a significant source of fructose (fruit sugar) so choose fruits such as apples, pears, cherries and plums. Berries are also a good choice owing to their high antioxidant content, for example blueberries, raspberries and strawberries.

Wholegrains, the outer husk of which has not been removed by processing, are a good source of unrefined carbohydrate. In the book there are recipes using buckwheat, brown basmati rice, pearl barley and quinoa, as these contain lots of minerals and vitamins.

Beans and pulses are admirably well-balanced foods. They are a good source of protein, complex carbohydrates, fibre and minerals, and are low in fat. Sprouting beans makes them particularly nutritious, as sprouts are full of enzymes; mung beans, usually eaten as bean sprouts, have been found to be rich in antioxidants.

Soya products, such as soya beans, tofu, miso and tempeh are excellent sources of vegetable protein. Soya protein can decrease LDL, the 'bad' cholesterol, by as much as 10-20%.

Nuts and seeds are nutrient-dense and contain essential fats, protein and some fibre. The best nuts are those with a higher proportion of monounsaturated fatty acids, such as hazelnuts, pecans and almonds. A recent study found that supplementing the diet with almonds not only helped people to lose weight but also enabled Type 1 diabetics to reduce their medication.

All this shows that changing eating habits, even a little, can bring about significant changes into our health and that of the entire family. Knowing what foods go together to make healthier dishes without sacrificing flavour can help us prevent cancers, keep diabetes at bay, control weight and cholesterol levels, and lower blood pressure. We can do this, ourselves, every day and this book we hope will guide you and your family successfully down the path of good health.

wok

skewers

whisk

skimmer

melon
baller

chopping
board

honey
dipper

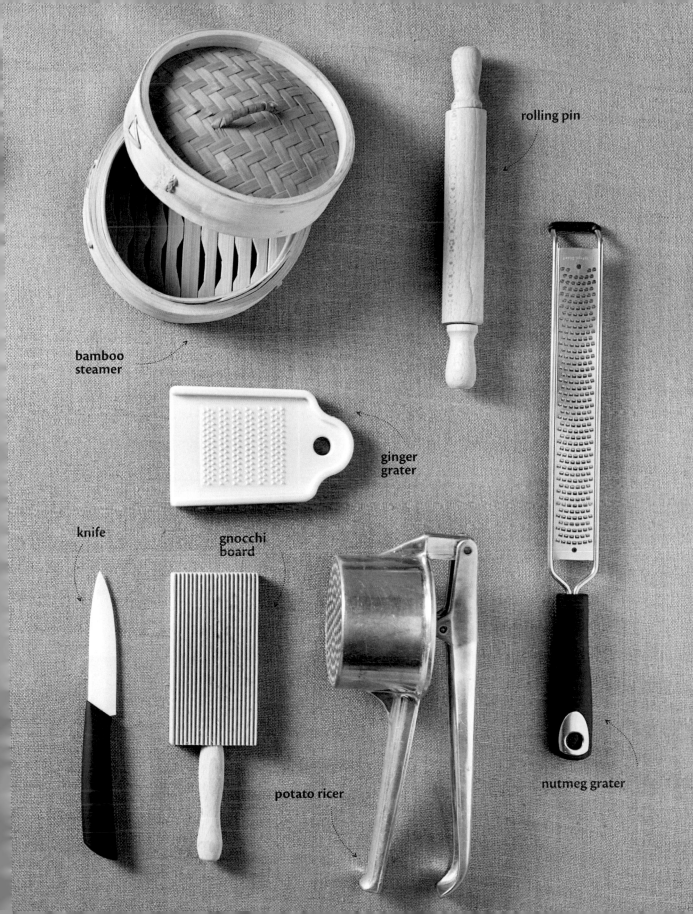

rolling pin

bamboo
steamer

ginger
grater

knife

gnocchi
board

potato ricer

nutmeg grater

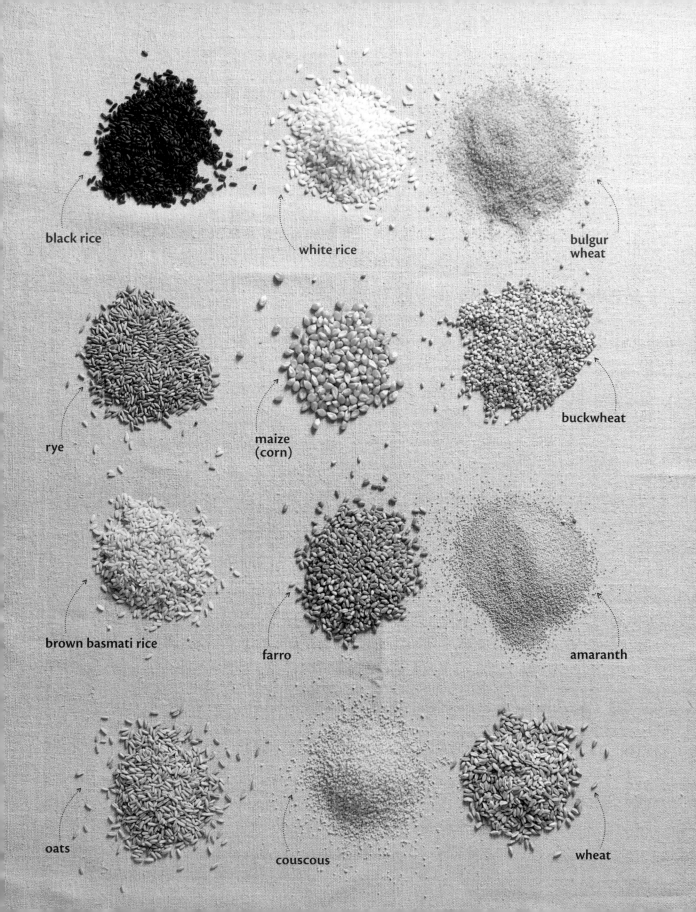

black rice

white rice

bulgur wheat

rye

maize (corn)

buckwheat

brown basmati rice

farro

amaranth

oats

couscous

wheat

whole grain barley

millet

cereals

Not only rice and wheat:
different grains have been
rediscovered in recent years,
such as farro, spelt, oats, millet
and many others. Tasty, versatile
and wholesome grains.

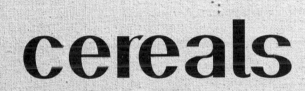

basmati rice

quinoa

wild rice

CEREAL GRAINS

THE MENTION OF cereals commonly makes people think of bread, pasta, breakfast cereals and all the other derivatives of wheat used in baked products, etc. with the addition of rice and maize, commonly referred to as corn. But there are other cereals that have formed the staple of the human diet for thousands of years all over the world: millet, barley, oats, rye, and pseudocereals such as buckwheat, amaranth and quinoa.

Cereals provide nourishment by making available to us a large proportion of the carbohydrates we need to be active and to think, in the form of starch. Only whole grain cereals, and the flours produced from them, actively provide precious nutritious substances that can be absorbed by our bodies in a balanced manner.

For millennia and in every traditional culture, cereal grains were the staple food for whole populations, and were accompanied not only by vegetables, but also by pulses, nuts, seeds and a small amount of animal protein in the form of eggs, cheese, fish and, only occasionally, meat. These were the true, archetypal foods of the ancient civilisations; one need only think of barley bread in Greece, mixed grain (millet, barley, farro) polenta in

Ancient Rome and rice in the Far East. When cereals were our main source of sustenance, obesity, cardio-vascular diseases, blood sugar and lipid imbalances and gastrointestinal tract ailments were relatively uncommon, while they are practically endemic today, and not only in Western countries.

The micronutrients found in whole grains carry out an important function: they improve the immune system, reduce inflammatory processes and help to protect cells against free radicals. Moreover, fibre encourages proper functioning of the digestive system and its soluble parts nourishes intestinal flora.

cereals that keep cholesterol under control

Only whole grain cereals are helpful, because the substances that lower cholesterol (fibre, phytosterols and niacin) are mainly present in the bran. Oats (groats with only the husk removed, not quick-cooking oats) are the quintessential cholesterol-lowering cereal. Whole barley is also beneficial, as are the so-called pseudocereals, such as buckwheat, quinoa and amaranth.

TABLE OF CEREAL COOKING TIMES

	cooking time in minutes	soaking time	volume of cooking water (parts liquid for one part cereal)
amaranth	30-40	–	2.5
oat groats	50	6 hours	3
quick-cooking oats	30	–	2
farro	60	6 hours	2.5
pearl farro	30		2
wheat	60	8 hours	3
buckwheat	15-20	–	2
khorasan wheat	60	8 hours	2.5
millet	30	–	2
barley groats (hulled or pot barley)	60	8 hours	3
pearl barley	40	2-3 hours	2
quinoa	20-25		2
brown rice	60		2
brown basmati rice	35	–	2
rye	60	8 hours	3

wheat

A cereal that is emblematic of the Mediterranean and part of practically every meal. The different varieties of *Triticum aestivum* (common or bread wheat) provide the flour for bread and all sweet and savoury baked products, while durum wheat provides the semolina used to make pasta. In the last two centuries wheat has overtaken all other crops grown in the world owing to its high yields and the fact that its flour is the best suited to industrial baking. It is the cereal with the highest content in gluten, a protein that gives elasticity to dough, helping it to rise. In addition to flour, it is also eaten in the form of pasta in typical dishes found in regional Italian cuisine. It is prepared In the Middle East in the form of bulgur wheat, and in North Africa as couscous. However it is mainly used to make bread, a staple food since the dawn of civilisation for its nutritional value and great symbolism.

Bulgur wheat. This is the name given to wheat berries that have been sprouted, parboiled and coarsely ground. It has a very high nutritional value. It forms the base of Lebanese cuisine, where it is used in countless dishes, from kibbeh (croquettes filled with pulses, vegetables or meat) to tabbouleh (a delicious summer salad made with onion, tomato and large amounts of parsley and lemon).

rye

This cereal is grown in cold climates. It is mainly used to make bread such as the typical Swedish knäckebröd (crispbread), or the German Schwarzbrot, dark bread enriched with fennel or cumin seeds. Rye is good for people with sedentary lifestyles because it promotes blood circulation, and its high fibre content stimulates bowel function. By soaking rye in water a sparkling and slightly alcoholic malt drink is made that was once very widespread throughout Eastern Europe known as kwas or kvas.

barley

Until the nineteenth century this was the most common food crop in the Mediterranean region. Barley mash served with pulses, vegetables and cheese was a typical dish of Ancient Greece; the loaves that were miraculously multiplied in the Gospels were made of barley; and the gladiators ate huge amounts of it to increase their strength. Barley is cooling for the gut, making it suitable for soups, minestrone and delicious summer salads.

maize (corn)

This is third most extensively farmed cereal by surface area, and forms the staple food of Mexico and the rest of Latin America, where it has always been combined with pulses. In the form of polenta, it became a staple food for many generations of farmers in Northern Italy. To improve its nutritional qualities, it required the addition of small amounts of protein (cheese, meat, fish or pulses), which gave rise to hearty and flavoursome dishes with salt cod and sauces made with pulses or cheese. Other uses include the addition of cooked sweetcorn kernels to salads and roasting or barbecuing corn on the cob. Maize does not contain gluten, which makes it one of the main cereals most suited for the diets of people with coeliac disease. It also has diuretic and laxative properties.

oats

Thriving even in cold climates, this cereal is extensively grown in Central and Northern Europe. It has the highest lipid content of any cereal and is also rich in protein. It has invigorating and slightly stimulating properties, and is therefore beneficial for people suffering from asthenia, depression or high blood pressure. Oats are widely used in Scotland and Ireland. They were often soaked in water and left on the stove overnight, so that the porridge would be ready for breakfast.

Rolled oats are among the most common cereal derivatives. They can be eaten without cooking, by leaving them to soak in water or milk, and are used to make muesli together with fresh and dried fruit, seeds and nuts. Rolled oats release small amounts of fat when cooked, and are perfect for thickening soups and for making sweet and savoury pastries, which will require almost no oil.

rice

This is the second most widely grown cereal in the world and is the staple crop for most of Asia. Italy has been the leading producer of quality rice in Europe since the fifteenth century. Rice comes in a great many varieties – long grain, medium grain and short grain varieties – and in different ways when cooked: there are also glutinous (sweet) Asian varieties that are suitable for desserts. But the most important difference is between polished 'white' rice and whole grain 'brown' rice, a delicate, balanced source of protein and energy-giving food with astringent, soothing and digestive properties. Rice lends itself to so many dishes and is at its best when cooked simply, in risotto, an iconic dish in Italian cuisine, and in elaborate and hearty dishes such as paella. It is ideal for sweet preparations such as the classic rice pudding.

quinoa

This grain is grown in the Andean regions of Chile and Peru. It is a very balanced source of protein, and actually contains less starch, more fat and more protein that other cereals. It is also a good source of calcium and iron, and is completely gluten-free. Before use, the kernels have to be carefully rinsed to remove the layers of saponin that protect them from parasites. It is cooked in a similar way as millet and its flour can be used to make cakes and biscuits.

According to traditional Chinese medicine, quinoa stands out for its stimulating and restorative properties. It is the only cereal that sustains the energy systems of the kidneys, making it very suitable for treating asthenia, backache and knee pain.

buckwheat

This is a hardy and fast-growing plant that tolerated poor soils and cold and damp climates, which is why it is very widely grown in northern Italy and now cultivated on a large scale in Poland and Russia. It is a very good source of energy and nutritious owing to its high content in essential amino acids, vitamins and minerals. It is most commonly used in the form of flour, which is dark and flavourful. Polenta taragna and pizzoccheri pasta are made from buckwheat flour, while the whole grains can be cooked by absorption or in soups. Another typical use is to make the Japanese soba or udon noodles.

amaranth

This grain is not from the *Gramineae* (true grass) family, but is a herbaceous species of the spinach family characterised by its deep red catkin-like inflorescences. The plant retains its appearance and vitality long after the harvest, which is why it was once held as a symbol of immortality by the Incas and Aztecs. Amaranth is suitable for people with coeliac disease as it is gluten-free. It is also particularly high in protein and calcium, which makes it perfect for wheat, rice and maize, and it is a good idea to use them together. Amaranth is used in soups and soufflé-type dishes, and can be added to bread dough.

farro

This grain belongs to the wheat family, and was the staple food for the ancient inhabitants of the Italian Peninsula and an iconic cereal for the Romans; its Italian name, farro, may be the origin of the word for flour, farina, and a soup made from farro was a very popular energy food. This cereal is hardy and withstands the cold. It is the chief ingredient of Tuscan soup dishes. It is also ideal for salads and to make timbales and rissoles. It is a good source of energy and has antioxidant properties.

millet

This is a cereal that really should be rediscovered. It is an energy-giving food that is also digestive and diuretic, and ideal for people suffering from debilitating health conditions or whose work involves intense intellectual activity. Completely gluten-free, it is ideal for use when weaning babies and can be considered a type of beauty product for skin, hair, nails and tooth enamel. Other than in soups, its agglutinating ability makes it suitable for pies, soufflé-type dishes and croquettes. Moreover, it is relatively quick to cook and has a delicate flavour that makes it versatile in the kitchen.

BULGUR WHEAT WITH BROAD BEANS AND COURGETTES

3-4 small courgettes

¼ teaspoon turmeric

1 teaspoon lemon juice

1 pinch sweet paprika

300 g bulgur wheat

2 tablespoons extra virgin olive oil

2 tablespoons white wine

1 teaspoon chives

650 ml vegetable stock

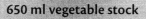

1-2 cloves garlic

salt

200 g cooked broad beans

1 Heat the stock with the turmeric and bulgur. Season with salt and boil for 10 minutes. Leave to stand, covered.	**2** Cut the courgettes first into 4 pieces, then chop into small pieces.	**3** Sauté for a few minutes in a frying pan with oil and garlic.
4 In 1 tbsp of oil brown the garlic and sauté the broad beans. Deglaze with the wine. Season with salt and the paprika.	**5** Transfer the cooked beans to a bowl and add the lemon and chopped chives.	**6** Add the courgette and bulgur wheat. Mix well and serve.

AMARANTH GARDENER'S STYLE

1 shallot

1 carrot

2 artichokes

300 g amaranth

600 ml vegetable stock

200 g shelled peas

salt

extra virgin olive oil

1

2

3

4

1 Clean the artichokes by removing the harder outer leaves and all but the top of the stalk.

2 Also remove the thorns by cutting off the top of the leaves with a knife. Cut the artichokes into pieces.

3 Peel the shallot (can be substituted with ¼ onion) and chop finely.

4 Rub the carrot clean with a brush without peeling, then dice.

5   Chop the parsley (this is optional and can be added to the amaranth according to preference).

6   Use a heavy-bottomed saucepan to brown the vegetables in 1 tbsp of oil for 5 minutes.

7   Add the amaranth to the mixed vegetables and toast by mixing with a wooden spoon for 1 minute.

8   Add the stock and cook for 25-30 minutes. Before serving, season with salt and drizzle with oil. If preferred, add 1 tbsp of chopped parsley.

TASTY SUMMER BARLEY

extra virgin olive oil

200 g peas

300 g pearl barley

salt

1 tablespoon salted capers

1 handful pitted black olives

¼ teaspoon turmeric

1 red pepper

vinegar

1 handful mixed herbs

2 carrots

1 clove garlic

1 spring onion

1 Cook the barley in 750 ml of salted water with the turmeric.

2 When cooked, spread it out in a dish to allow it to cool quickly.

3-4 Dice the carrot and boil in water with salt and 2 tbsp of vinegar.

Barley is typically considered a refreshing cereal and particularly soothing for the gut, so it is very suitable to be eaten in summer.

5

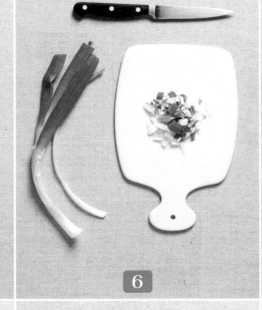

6

7

8

9

10

5	Meanwhile, dice the red pepper.	6	Chop the spring onion with a paring knife.	7	Sauté it in a frying pan with 1 tbsp of oil, the garlic, carrot and red pepper.
8	Add the peas and cook until tender.	9	Finely chop the herbs with the capers and olives.	10	Mix the barley with the other ingredients and leave to stand. Serve at room temperature.

FENNEL AND SAFFRON RICE

1 clove garlic

½ onion

3 small fennel bulbs

2 tablespoons pitted black olives

1 handful pistachios

1 sachet ground saffron

300 g brown rice, long grain

125 ml chopped tomatoes

extra virgin olive oil

coarse sea salt

1 Cook the brown rice in 600 ml of water for 50 minutes.	**2** Sweat the chopped onion in 2 tbsp of oil. Peel the fennel and cut each bulb into 8 pieces.	**3** Add to the onion and cook for 5 minutes.
4 Deglaze pan with some white wine and raise the heat. Add the sliced black olives.	**5** Add the tomato, season with salt, and cook for 10 minutes. Add the saffron dissolved in warm water.	**6** Cook for 10 minutes more. Serve the rice very hot, decorate with chopped pistachios.

BUCKWHEAT CROQUETTES WITH BEETROOT SAUCE

1 teaspoon parsley

1 roasted beetroot

1 pinch nutmeg

½ pot Greek yoghurt

250 g buckwheat

coarse sea salt

1 pinch black pepper

1 sprig thyme

1 egg

extra virgin olive oil

1 Dice the roasted and peeled beetroot.

2 Season with salt, pepper and olive oil.

3 Blend with the yoghurt.

4 Sweat the chopped onion well in 2 tbsp of oil until golden.

5 Add the buckwheat (rinsed and drained) and brown quickly while mixing gently.

6 Add 500 ml water or vegetable stock, bring to a boil and cook over a low heat.

7   Transfer the buckwheat to a bowl, separate the grains with a fork and leave to cool.

8   Add the egg to the buckwheat and mix.

9   Chop the herbs and add.

10   Season with the nutmeg and salt, and mix. Blend the grain mixture.

11   Wet your hands lightly, then form croquettes with the mixture.

12   Fry in very hot oil until crunchy. Serve with the sauce.

FARRO WITH PUMPKIN CREAM AND PEAS

1 teaspoon
thyme leaves

1 cup peas

extra virgin olive oil

1 onion

300 g pearl farro

1 slice pumpkin

salt

1 litre vegetable stock

1 Cook the farro in the vegetable stock for 25-30 minutes.	**2** Finely chop the onion and brown in a frying pan with a little oil and the peas for 5 minutes.
3 Add the diced pumpkin and cook through. Add vegetable stock if required. Adjust the seasoning to taste.	**4** When cooked, the pumpkin should have a creamy consistency. Add the farro to the pumpkin cream and serve hot.

BARLEY WITH ASPARAGUS

1.5 litres vegetable stock

2 pinches ground saffron

1 small carrot

salt

300 g pearl barley

1 shallot

1 bunch asparagus

1 small onion

extra virgin olive oil

1	Heat the stock. Slice the asparagus, setting aside the tips with 2 cm of stalk.	2	Dice the carrot and onion. Sweat the vegetables in a little oil for 5 minutes.	3	Add the barley and toast for several minutes.
4	Gradually add the stock. After 30 minutes, turn off the heat, add the saffron, and leave to stand, covered.	5	Finely chop the shallot. Brown in a frying pan with a little oil.	6	Add the asparagus tips, season with salt, cook for 5 minutes, and serve.

RICE NOODLES WITH STIR-FRIED VEGETABLES

2 spring onions with their leaves

¼ Savoy cabbage

3 slices ginger

1 red pepper

1 clove garlic

250 g rice noodles

1 yellow pepper

toasted sesame oil (or olive oil)

soy sauce

1 Thinly slice the cabbage lengthwise.	**2** Peel the spring onions and thinly slice lengthwise.	**3** Clean the peppers and cut into thin strips.
4 Use a wide-bladed knife to crush the garlic and ginger.	**5** Heat oil in a wok on a high heat with the garlic and ginger.	**6** Add the cabbage and stir-fry for 3 minutes.

7 Add the spring onion and cook for another 5 minutes. Remove the vegetables.	**8** Add more oil, when very hot, stir-fry the peppers for 5 minutes.	**9** Bring water to a boil and add the noodles. Add a little salt and cook for 3 minutes.
10 Drain the cooked but still firm noodles in a colander.	**11** Add noodles to the wok with the vegetables and stir-fry so flavours blend.	**12** Remove from the heat and season the noodles and vegetables with soy sauce.

COLOURFUL FARRO SALAD

balsamic vinegar

½ red pepper

200 g cooked
chickpeas

3 sprigs thyme

200 g French
(green) beans

300 g farro

extra virgin olive oil

1 aubergine, sliced
and grilled

1 clove garlic

coarse sea salt

1 Cut the aubergine slices into small pieces and season with the oil and salt, and oregano (optional).	**2** Boil the beans for 10-15 minutes and set aside their cooking water.
3-4 Cook the farro in the bean cooking water. Meanwhile, cut the beans into small pieces and season with oil, salt and a splash of balsamic vinegar.	Farro is an ideal cereal for use in salads. Flavourful and filling, it makes a perfect, energy-giving breakfast.

| 5 | 6 |
| 7 | 8 |

<table>
</table>

5   Dice the pepper and sauté in a frying pan with oil and garlic, allowing it to remain firm and crisp. Adjust the seasoning to taste.

6   Fry the chickpeas in a frying pan with 1 tbsp of oil until golden. Remove from the heat and season with 2 pinches of paprika (optional).

7   Separate the farro grains well and transfer to a salad bowl. Mix with the vegetables and chickpeas.

8   Season with salt, all the thyme leaves and a splash of extra virgin olive oil.

LENTIL AND MILLET SOUP

extra virgin olive oil

100 g French (green) beans

2 carrots

200 g millet

¼ pumpkin

salt

1 onion

½ kg Swiss chard

100 g lentils

1 Dice the onion and carrots. Peel the pumpkin. Cut the pumpkin and beans into pieces.	**2** Wash the chard, removing any soil, and coarsely chop with a knife.	**3** Sauté onion, carrot, pumpkin and beans with 2 tbsp of oil. Season with salt and cook for 7-8 minutes.
4 Add the lentils and cook for several minutes. Add the chopped chard.	**5** After 2 minutes, add the rinsed millet and toast. Add 500 ml of water and cook for 30 minutes.	**6** Remove from the heat, season with salt and 2 tbsp of oil and leave to rest for 10 minutes before serving.

PUMPKIN AND RYE GNOCCHI

2 tbsp vegetarian pesto

2 tablespoons tomato purée

½ onion

2 tablespoons wheat flour

2 eggs

4 tablespoons rye flour

500 g pumpkin, peeled and roasted

1 head broccoli

2 tablespoons extra virgin olive oil

salt

1 Pass the roasted pumpkin through a potato ricer. Add the eggs.	**2** Add the two types of flour. Mix well until the mixture forms a smooth paste. Leave to stand for at least 30 minutes.
3 Divide the broccoli into florets. Peel the stalk and cut into pieces.	**4** Heat the oil in a frying pan and brown the chopped onion. Add a little chilli pepper (optional). Add the broccoli and mix well, allowing it to absorb the flavour.

5   Add the tomato purée diluted with a little water, season with salt. Cover and cook until tender, adding water if necessary.

6   Turn off the heat and add the pesto to the broccoli.

7   Use a spoon and a knife to form gnocchi a little smaller than a walnut in size. Slide them straight from the spoon into boiling salted water.

8   When they float remove after 3 minutes. Drop into the pan with the broccoli, stir gently for 2 minutes to allow them to absorb the flavour. Drizzle with oil when serving.

CAVATELLI PASTA WITH ROMANESCO

extra virgin olive oil

1 onion

500 g romanesco or broccoli

10 sun-dried tomatoes in oil

2 pinches chilli powder

300 g durum wheat flour (semolina)

125 ml white wine

coarse sea salt

2 tablespoons grated vegetarian ricotta cheese

2 tablespoons pine nuts, lightly toasted

1. Mix the semolina with 1 tbsp of oil, the wine and a little lukewarm water. Work it into a dough, then knead into a soft, and elastic ball. Cover and leave to rest.

2. Wash the romanesco. Use a knife to cut it into florets.

3. Thinly slice the onion and sweat with 1 tbsp of oil and the chilli. Add the romanesco, season with salt and cook until tender, adding a little water if necessary.

4. After 10 minutes, transfer to a pot and add the sun-dried tomatoes cut into thin strips. Turn off the heat and cover with a lid.

5   Divide the dough into 8 pieces. Roll each piece into strings about the length of a little finger.

6   Cut into 2 cm lengths, then press each piece with two fingers to obtain a shape like a mini hot dog bun.

7   Bring water to the boil and add salt. Cook the pasta for about 10 minutes, then drain and sauté in a frying pan with the vegetables.

8   Before serving, sprinkle the pasta with pine nuts and grated cheese. Finish with a drizzle of oil.

MISO SOUP
WITH VERMICELLI

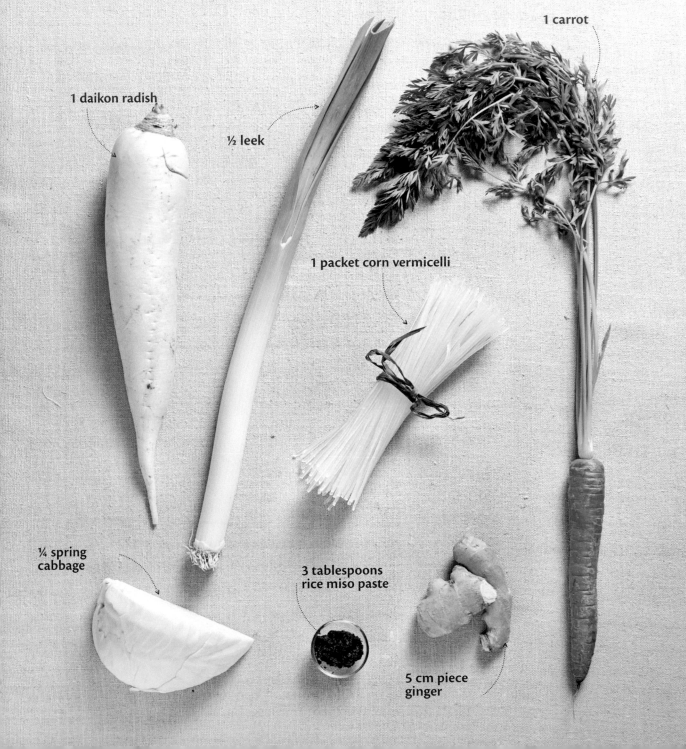

1 carrot

1 daikon radish

½ leek

1 packet corn vermicelli

¼ spring
cabbage

3 tablespoons
rice miso paste

5 cm piece
ginger

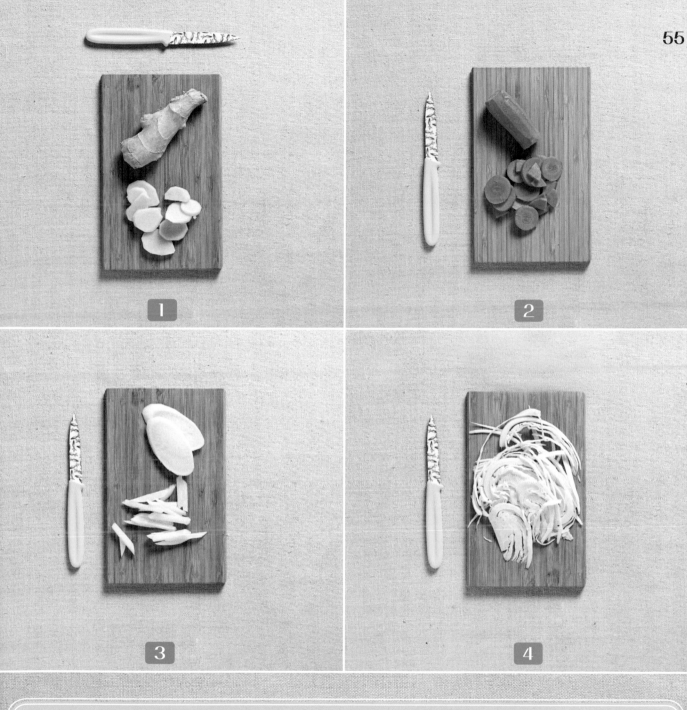

1		2	

3		4	

1   Peel the ginger and slice into rounds.

2   Slice the carrot into rounds, then quarter each piece.

3-4   Peel the daikon and cut into small batons. Slice the cabbage thinly.

The corn vermicelli, available in Asian food shops, can be replaced with buckwheat soba noodles.

5 Peel and finely slice the leek.

6 Place all the prepared ingredients in a pot with 1.5 litres of water. Bring to a boil. Cover and cook for 15 minutes.

7 Then add the vermicelli to the pot and cook until soft.

8 Before serving, dissolve the miso paste in a little of the liquid, then add it to the soup without allowing it to boil.

COLOURFUL SWEETCORN SALAD

150 g cooked sweetcorn kernels

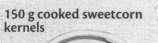

balsamic vinegar

1 clove garlic

salt

1 head escarole or other endive

soy sauce

1 head radicchio

10 walnuts

1 head broccoli

extra virgin olive oil

1	Gently wash the salad leaves and dry thoroughly.	**2**	Wash the broccoli, discard the woody part of the stalk and divide into florets.
3	Heat 1 tbsp of extra virgin olive oil in a frying pan and brown the garlic for about 1 minute.	**4**	Add the broccoli florets, season with salt and cook for 6-7 minutes, stirring often. The broccoli should remain crisp and bright green.

| 5 | Crack the walnuts and divide the kernels into 4 pieces, taking care not to shatter them. | 6 | Break up the salad leaves by hand into a salad bowl. | 7-8 | Add the broccoli, sweetcorn and walnut pieces. |
| 9 | Make a vinaigrette with 2 tbsp of oil, ½ tbsp of soy sauce and ½ tbsp of balsamic vinegar. | 10 | Dress the salad with the vinaigrette and serve. | | In Chinese medicine, corn has diuretic properties and regulates digestion. It is also gluten-free. |

BROCCOLI CREAM PIE

1 pinch chilli powder

2 tablespoons pine nuts

600 g broccoli

250 g whole grain farro flour

1 clove garlic

extra virgin olive oil

2 tablespoons grated vegetarian cheese

salt

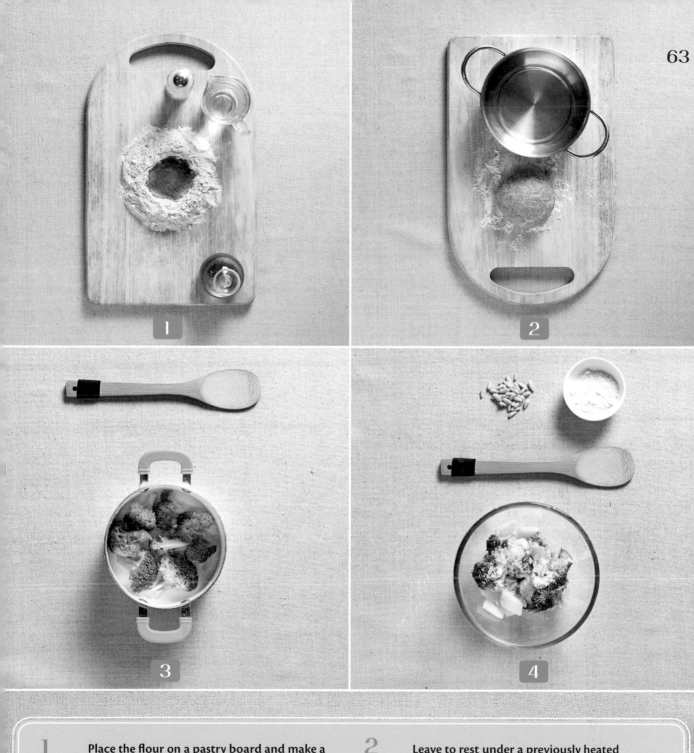

1 Place the flour on a pastry board and make a well in the centre. Place 3 tbsp of oil, a pinch of salt and about 75 ml of hot water inside the well. Knead until the resulting dough is elastic.

2 Leave to rest under a previously heated saucepan turned upside down.

3 Cook the broccoli florets and sliced garlic in a saucepan in two fingers of water.

4 Transfer the broccoli to a bowl and combine with the pine nuts, cheese and chilli.

5 Blend the broccoli, pine nuts, cheese and chilli mixture to a thick cream.

6 Roll out ⅔ of the dough into a thin pastry sheet. Line a 26 cm diameter greased pie mould with the pastry.

7 Place the broccoli cream filling directly over the pastry in the mould.

8 Cover with the remaining pastry and fold in edges. Prick the surface with a fork, brush with oil and bake at 180°C for 25 minutes.

MUSHROOM AND OAT PIE

250 g button mushrooms

1 sprig thyme

2 tablespoons
coarse cornmeal

3 tablespoons extra
virgin olive oil

coarse sea salt

300 g pinhead oatmeal
(steel-cut rolled oats)

1 carrot

1 small leek

250 ml vegetable stock

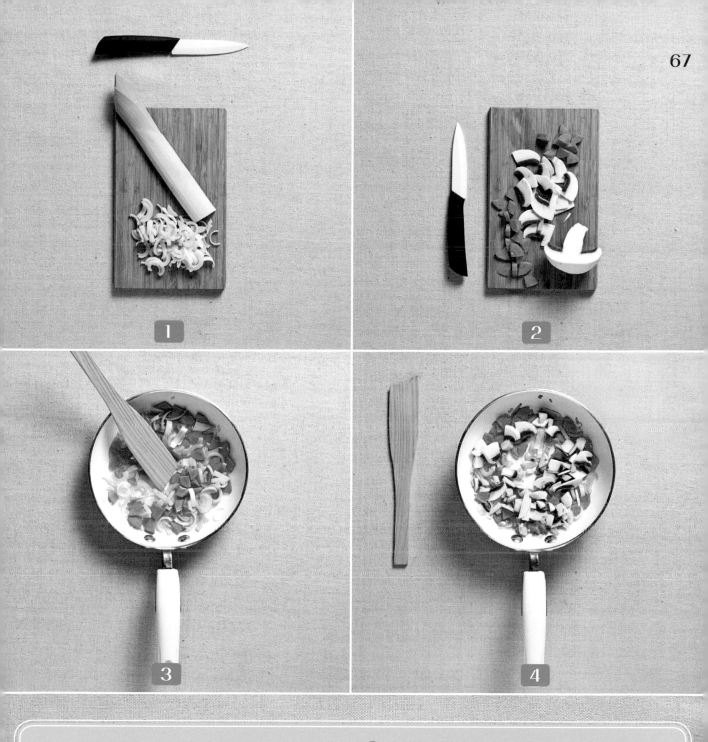

1. Cut the leek in half and finely slice on a chopping board.

2. Chop the carrot into small pieces. Slice the mushrooms after trimming off the stem bottoms.

3. Sweat the leek and carrot in 2 tbsp of extra virgin olive oil in a large frying pan.

4. After 5 minutes, add the mushrooms to the pan. Season with salt and cook for 7-8 minutes.

5 Add the oatmeal to the pan and toast lightly.

6 Add the thyme and vegetable stock, and cook for another 5 minutes.

7 Grease a baking dish with oil to prevent the pie from sticking, and dust with cornmeal.

8 Spread the mixture in a layer 2 cm thick, sprinkle again with cornmeal and drizzle with oil. Bake at 200°C for 10 minutes.

PUMPKIN AND MILLET PIE

¼ pumpkin

1 onion

salt

4 sage leaves

500 g cooked millet
(from 200 g raw millet)

extra virgin olive oil

rosemary

1 clove garlic

1 Chop the onion and brown with the sage leaves, garlic and 2 tbsp of oil.	**2** After 5 minutes, add the peeled and diced pumpkin. Mix well so that it absorbs the flavours.	**3** Remove from heat and remove garlic and sage. Add the millet, mix and season with salt.
4 Add 250 ml of water (or vegetable stock) and cook through.	**5** Grease a dish, spread the millet out in a 1.5-2 cm layer.	**6** Finish with oil and rosemary, then bake at 200°C until golden and serve.

SWEET AND SPICY COUSCOUS

¼ pineapple,
very ripe

200 g couscous

3 cardamom
pods

½ tablespoon
cane sugar

½ vanilla
pod

1 tablespoon
ginger juice

2 tablespoons
desiccated coconut

100 g fresh
dates

2 kiwifruit

1 untreated
lemon

280 g
strawberries

100 g raisins

1	Bring water to the boil with the split vanilla pod, a small piece of lemon peel and the crushed cardamom. Cover and leave to stand.	2	Rinse the raisins and drain. Chop the dates with a paring knife.
3	Transfer them to a bowl with the couscous. While still very hot add the infused and strained water. Cover and leave the couscous to swell for 10 minutes.	4	Prepare individual moulds by spraying the inside with a little water and dusting with desiccated coconut.

5 Fill with the couscous and level off so the top is even.

6 Peel and grate the ginger.

7 Extract 1 tbsp of juice by squeezing the grated pulp.

8 Peel or trim the pineapple, strawberries and kiwifruit and cut into dice.

9 Dress the fruit salad with the sugar and ginger juice.

10 Turn out the couscous from the moulds and serve with the fruit salad.

APPLE AND QUINOA PIE

2 tablespoons extra virgin olive oil

3 tablespoons rice malt syrup

200 g quinoa flour

2 eating apples

2 tablespoons toasted flaked almonds

½ teaspoon untreated orange peel

1 pinch salt

1 pinch ground cinnamon

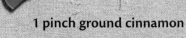

3 tablespoons Seville orange marmalade

1 teaspoon yeast

75 g vegetarian ricotta cheese

1	
2	
3	
4	

1 Combine the flour, ricotta, oil, malt syrup, salt, yeast, orange peel and a little warm water and knead into a dough. Leave the dough to rest for 20 minutes in the fridge wrapped in a damp cloth.

3 Use one sheet to line a 20 cm diameter pie mould.

2 Cook the sliced apple with 2 tbsp of water and the cinnamon for 5 minutes, then leave to stand. Divide the dough into halves and roll out both halves into thin sheets.

4 Spread a layer of marmalade over the pastry.

5 Make a layer of apples and toasted flaked almonds on top.

6 Cover the apple and almond filling with the second pastry sheet.

7 Press the pastry edges to seal and prick with a fork to prevent swelling when baked.

8 Glaze the crust by brushing with a little marmalade diluted with water. Bake in a hot oven at 180°C for 45-50 minutes.

MILLET TIMBALES WITH RASPBERRY SAUCE

400 ml almond milk

lemon peel

250 g raspberries

½ vanilla pod

1 handful toasted chopped almonds

200 g millet

½ tablespoon cornflour + extra for dusting

1 handful raisins

250 ml clear apple juice

1 tablespoon multi-flower honey

120 g rice malt syrup

1. Cook the millet in the milk with the lemon peel and vanilla for 20 minutes.

2. Remove from the heat and discard the lemon peel and vanilla. Add the malt syrup and mix well.

3. Add the almonds and rinsed raisins. Incorporate well.

4. Lightly grease 4 x 10-12 cm diameter individual moulds with oil and dust with some cornflour.

5 Fill the moulds with a 2 cm layer of the millet, raisin and almond mixture. Bake at 180°C for about 15 minutes.

6 Meanwhile, prepare the sauce in a pan: dissolve the ½ tbsp cornflour in the apple juice.

7 Add the raspberries and bring to the boil while stirring constantly.

8 Remove from the heat, sweeten with the honey and blend. Turn out the millet timbales and serve with the sauce. They can be decorated with fresh raspberries.

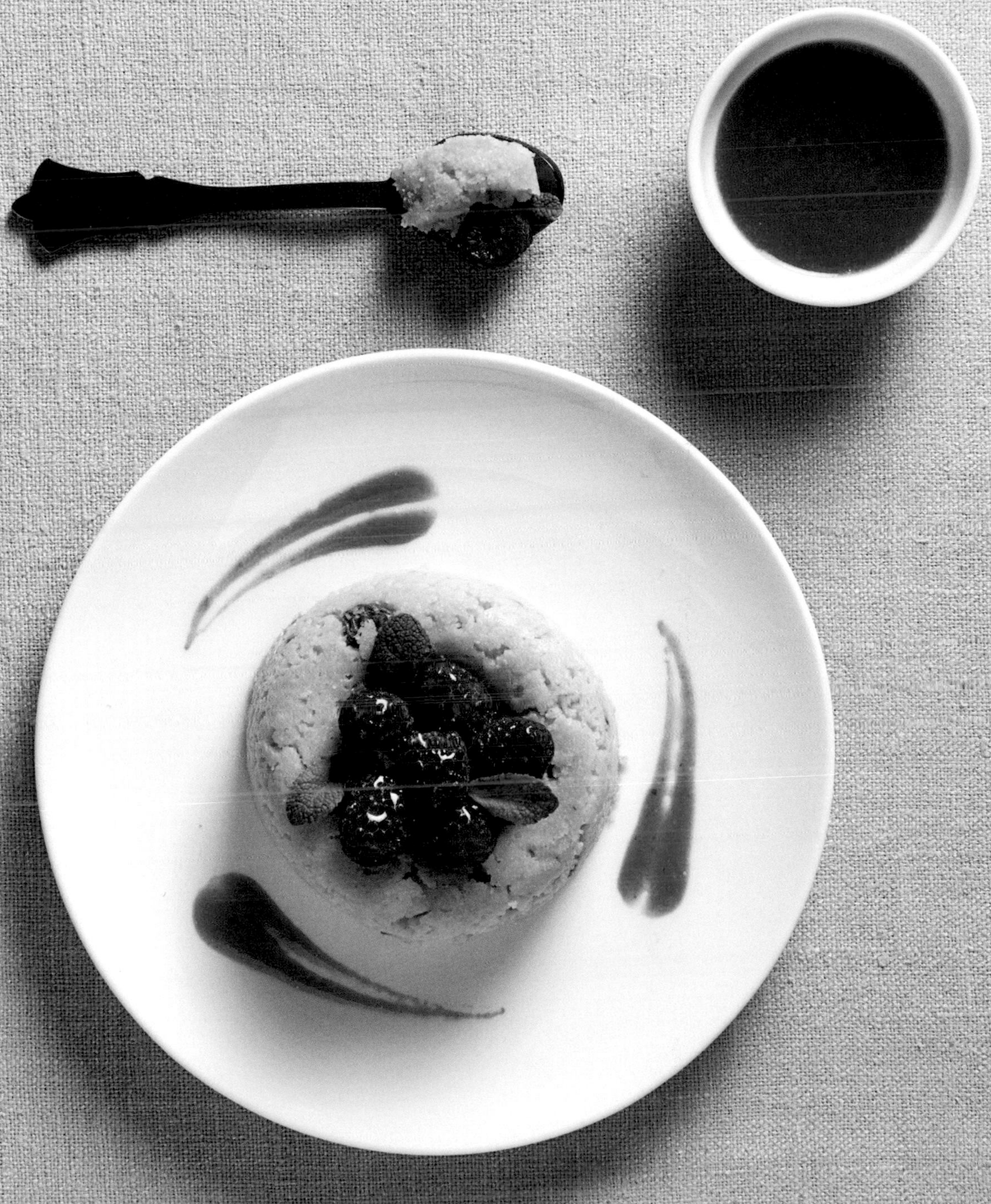

SWEET POLENTA

150 g coarse cornmeal
(polenta)

100 g organic dried
apricots

450 ml water

50 g toasted hazelnuts

5 tablespoons multi-flower
honey

1	Prepare the polenta: bring water to the boil, add the flour and stir for 10 minutes.	**2** Quarter the hazelnuts and cut dried apricots into small pieces.

1. Prepare the polenta: bring water to the boil, add the flour and stir for 10 minutes.

2. Quarter the hazelnuts and cut dried apricots into small pieces.

3. Away from the heat, mix in the apricot and hazelnut pieces.

4. After 5 minutes, add the honey to the polenta and incorporate well.

5. Transfer the mixture to a heat-resistant dish and spread out in a 1-2 cm thick layer. Leave to cool.

6. Cut the hazelnut and almond polenta into squares and serve.

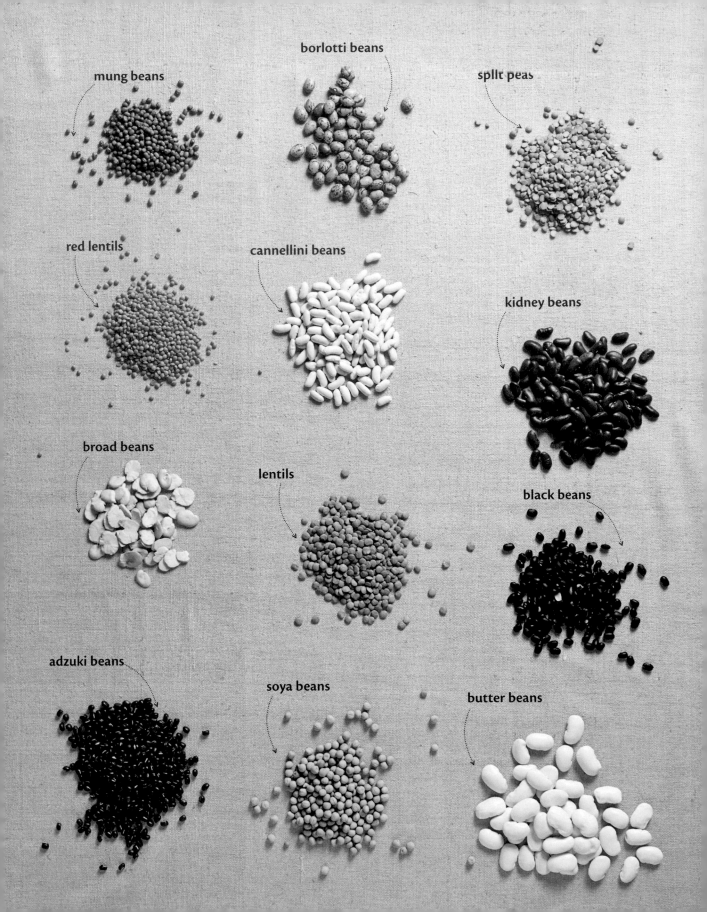

mung beans

borlotti beans

spllt peas

red lentils

cannellini beans

kidney beans

broad beans

lentils

black beans

adzuki beans

soya beans

butter beans

peanuts

pulses

Tasty, versatile and varied,
pulses are a major source
not only of proteins,
but also of vitamins
and trace elements.

fresh peas

fresh broad beans

PULSES

PULSES (peas, chickpeas, broad beans, haricot beans, lentils, soya beans, lupini beans) are seeds from plants belonging to the *Leguminosae* or pea family and are a nutritional gold mine. For many peoples of the world over the centuries, pulses have been the only alternative source of protein to meat, and it is interesting to note that among these populations, the incidence of cardiovascular diseases and cancer has not been as high as in richer and more meat-consuming societies. Until the turn of the twentieth century many Mediterranean countries on average would eat fifty grams of pulses per day. The current rate is ten grams per day and continues to fall. They are mistakenly blamed for being fattening, taking too long to cook, being difficult to digest, causing bloating, and as a result are now rarely seen on our tables. However, they deserve greater attention in our kitchens.

Pulses are actually very high in protein, and the amino acids they contain are a perfect complement for whole grain cereals. They are the food group with the highest fibre content, and are also rich in trace elements (copper, manganese, zinc, iodine, iron), vitamins such as B1, B2 and B3, and contain no cholesterol.

TABLE OF PULSE COOKING TIMES

	cooking time in minutes	soaking time
chickpeas	90-120	12-24 hours
beans	60-120	12-24 hours
broad beans	90-120	12-24 hours
lentils	30-80	0-6 hours
split peas	60	4 hours
adzuki beans	60-75	8 hours
mung beans	45-60	6 hours
black beans	120	24 hours

carminative and stimulating effect on digestion. Another trick is not to have too large a quantity in the same meal. Pulses should therefore be eaten regularly, so as to accustom the gut to assimilating them.

Using germinated pulses, the best known of which are bean sprouts, typically mung beans, normally found at greengrocers' and supermarkets, is another way to prepare dishes full of vitality and flavour without having to cook them.

Another reason why we should increase our use of pulses is that, besides being good for our bodies, they are also good for the planet. The production of pulses requires ten times less resources compared to the production of meat and other animal proteins.

Moreover, pulses stabilise blood sugar levels, stimulate gastrointestinal transit, lower cholesterol levels and generally protect us from lifestyle diseases.

The only drawbacks are that they can cause trapped wind and that they can also be difficult to digest, but a little good sense is all you need if you want to fully enjoy all the virtues of these 'wonder seeds'. It is necessary to soak them (the time varies depending on size) and to change the water before cooking. They have to be thoroughly cooked (pulses that are still a little hard are indigestible) in water for the required time (see table) on low heat and with herbs such as bay leaf, sage and savory, or spices like fennel seeds, all of which have a

asian-style lentils

Gently scoop out the seeds of 1 pomegranate into a bowl and add 300 g of cooked lentils, the juice of 1 lemon, 2 tablespoons of chopped parsley and extra virgin olive oil. Mix and season with salt. Leave to stand for at least half an hour before serving.

chickpeas

Chickpeas have been used as food for about five thousand years. Chickpea plants have very deep roots, which allow the plant to withstand the driest climates. There is also a variety of black chickpeas that is grown in Apulia in Italy. Chickpeas have a high content in certain phytochemicals (saponins and glycosides) which are very effective in eliminating cholesterol through bowel movements, reducing risks linked to cardiovascular diseases and high cholesterol. Chickpeas should therefore be eaten regularly by people suffering from high blood pressure and obesity. They are also mildly laxative and have diuretic properties. They are also beneficial owing to their high content in trace elements: magnesium, calcium, phosphorous, iron and potassium. There are countless ways chickpeas can be used, such as in different stews, soups, fritters, etc.

broad beans

While not very popular in Europe today, these beans are commonly used in the Middle East and other parts of Asia. Broad beans are Britain's original bean, grown since the Iron Age. They were widely eaten in Ancient Greece and Rome and had important symbolic meaning: they were associated with the cult of the dead and played a part in religious rites to honour the dead. This particular association is perhaps due to the colour of the flowers of this plant, which are white with black markings, a combination that is quite rare in the plant world. They are high in protein, dietary fibre and minerals: potassium, phosphorous, calcium, sodium and iron. They have a restorative and diuretic effect and are a laxative owing to their fibre content. They are often served seasonally when fresh, combined with hard cheese. Dried broad beans are perfect for soups, stews, curries, dips, dhal, Moroccan bessara, Egyptian falafel and Puglian mashed beans with chicory.

lentils

In use since ancient times, lentils were already known in the seventh millennium BC. They are produced by drought-resistant plants that are perfectly suited to growing in semi-arid regions with a temperate climate. Lentils are rich in flavour and different properties because of their high content in protein, carbohydrate, minerals (potassium, phosphorous, magnesium, calcium. copper, iron), viamins (B1, B2, B3) and dietary fibre. They have antioxidant activity, are easy to digest, regulate gastrointestinal function, and are recommended in cases of anaemia and for women who are pregnant or breastfeeding. Lentils are at their best in soups, but are also perfect for adding flavour to stews. They are an energy-giving complement for cereals, and are ideal for making vegetarian sauces and appetising croquettes. They are the most useful of the pulses as they do not need soaking before cooking.

adzuki

These are small red beans that are commonly used in Japanese cuisine. They are a good source of minerals and have excellent nutritional properties. They are easily digested, diuretic and cleansing, and also help to keep the immune system in good working order. They are generally cooked with a piece of kombu seaweed or a bay leaf. The are a good accompaniment for pumpkin and can be used to make a tasty pâté. They are also used to make traditional Chinese and Japanese desserts.

peas

The origins of this plant go back to ancient times in Asia. Freshly picked peas are exquisite for their refreshing sweet flavour. They best withstand the deep-freezing process, which is the form in which they are widely used in Western countries, while they are popular dried or split in Asia. Fresh peas have few calories and are a good source of plant protein; they are high in potassium and also contain phosphorous, calcium, iron, vitamin C and B group vitamins. They have diuretic properties, stimulate gastrointestinal transit, strengthen the immune system and are a good source of iron in cases of anaemia. They also contain phytoestrogens, making them useful for relieving symptoms of menopause. Fresh peas are used as an accompaniment, combined with rice, in salads with cereals, in soups, in stews and sauces. Dried peas are used to prepare creams, purées, rissoles and timbales.

mung beans

Mung beans are often, mistakenly, known as "green soya beans". They are widely used in the form of sprouts, and are often found in pulse mixes for making soups. Because they are very small, their cooking time is relatively short (about 1 hour). They are also used in Asia to make bean thread or glass noodles. In Chinese medicine they are used to clear body heat and are a specific purgative for urinary tract ailments such as cystitis.

peanuts

While generally accepted as an oilseed, the peanut is actually a pulse. This plant is native to Brazil. Peanuts are sold commercially dry-roasted in order to rid them of any mould contamination and to prevent them from turning rancid quickly given their high oil content. In the countries where they are grown they are eaten boiled in soup, with other vegetables or pulses, or fried. They are a vital source of protein in Africa and form an essential part of the traditional diet. Another use is in the form of peanut butter, especially in the United States where it is used to make sweet and savoury preparations or simply spread over bread. Peanuts are rich in protein and oils, and contain magnesium, calcium and phosphorous. They also contain a lot of dietary fibre. Because they are highly nutritious, they are recommended for reduced energy levels or increased energy needs, such as breastfeeding mothers or people with very intense physical activity. There is a recipe containing peanuts on page 190.

beans

The white, black and red varieties all originated in the Americas, while black-eyed beans are native to Europe, Africa and Asia. They are used both fresh and dried. Dried beans are soaked in water to rehydrate before cooking. Green bean varieties, such as runner beans and French beans, are eaten with their pods. They are considered vegetables despite belonging to the bean family.

Beans are very nutritious and are a good source of plant protein. Combined with cereals (as is typical in all traditional styles of cuisine), they have a nutritional value similar to that of meat and other animal protein. Thanks to their high dietary fibre content they stimulate gastrointestinal transit and are useful in cases of constipation and haemorrhoids. In addition, they lower cholesterol and triglyceride levels, and also act to regulate blood sugar. The most common bean varieties generally available are red kidney, cannellini, borlotti and butter beans. They are featured in countless recipes, from stews to salads.

soya beans

Soya beans have formed a part of the Chinese diet since 3000 BC, while their use in Western countries is relatively recent (grown for the first time in 1929). Currently, they are mainly used for animal feed, and the world's largest producers are the United States and Brazil. They have a very high content in protein, essential oils, lecithin, vitamins and minerals, but they are not easy to use in their natural state, in other words, soaked and cooked like other vegetables. So, in order to use them today, we must turn to Oriental traditions that have made soya beans into a tasty and versatile food. The best known and most widely used derivative is soya milk. This is obtained by soaking the beans for 24 hours, then draining and blending the beans in three times their volume of water and cooking for 15 minutes. Everything is strained and the collected liquid is known as soya milk. This liquid is used as a drink, to make puddings and custards, and different types of sauces. The remaining pulp, known as okara, is used to make tasty rissoles, or added to the mixtures used to make crackers or breadsticks in order to increase their protein content.

Miso. Fermented soya beans with added rice or barley make miso, an extraordinarily rich source of protein and lactic acid bacteria and enzymes, which are beneficial for digestion and to strengthen our intestinal flora. it is used to flavour soups and to make appetising sauces to accompany cereals or vegetables. It is always added at the end of the cooking process so as to preserve its properties.

Soy sauce and tamari These sauces are obtained by fermenting soya beans for at least 3 months in wooden barrels with salt and yeast. To make Japanese shoyu, wheat is also added, giving the sauce a more delicate flavour. Tamari, on the other hand, is gluten-free. They are used to flavour vegetables, fish, seeds, and as an ingredient in other different sauces. Chinese medicine considers soy sauce to have cooling and purgative properties.

CREAMY BEAN DIPS

1 tablespoon tahini

2 bay leaves

salt

1 cooked beetroot

2 sprigs thyme

300 g cooked cannellini beans

1 tablespoon soy sauce

extra virgin olive oil

1 sprig rosemary

vinegar

1 clove garlic

1 tablespoon miso paste

200 g black beans

2 pinches freshly ground black pepper

3 pinches chilli powder

1	For the red cannellini bean hummus: coarsely chop the peeled beetroot.
2	Remove the green core from the garlic, then chop half the clove.
3	Season the beans and beetroot with 2-3 tablespoons of oil and the vinegar, pepper, soy sauce and tahini.
4	Blend to a cream using a hand-held blender.

5	Add the chopped garlic and chives (optional) at the end. Season with salt and serve.

6	For the bean pâté: soak the black beans for 12 hours, then boil with the herbs for about 75 minutes.

7	Drain and transfer to a bowl. Set aside a little of the cooking water to dilute the pâté if necessary. Combine with the miso paste, 1 slice of garlic (chopped), chilli powder and 1 tbsp of soy sauce.

8	Blend together. Before serving, season with a little balsamic vinegar and extra virgin olive oil (optional). Serve the dips to accompany crudités.

COURGETTE AND BEAN
PATÉ SANDWICHES

2 large courgettes

2 pinches oregano

extra virgin olive oil

350 g fresh broad
beans, peeled

1 tablespoon pine
nuts

salt

balsamic vinegar

3 tablespoons grated
hard vegetarian cheese

2 sprigs mint

1   Clean the courgettes and slice lengthwise.

2   Grill on a griddle pan with raised ridges, and season with salt, oil, balsamic vinegar and oregano.

3   Parboil the beans for 3 minutes in boiling water. Blend in a liquidiser with the other ingredients, except the oil and cheese; add these at the end.

4   Cut the courgette slices into 3-4 cm squares and make into sandwiches with the bean pâté filling.

PULSE DIPS

200 g red lentils

1 clove garlic

40 g cooked chickpeas

8 tablespoons extra virgin olive oil

1 teaspoon paprika

salt

soy sauce

200 g dried broad beans, split (soaked for 6 hours)

parsley

100 g walnut kernels

1 teaspoon curry powder

2 shallots

¼ teaspoon chilli powder

80 g cashew nuts

balsamic vinegar

1 bay leaf

500 ml vegetable stock

1 lemon

2 onions

1 For the lentil dip: rinse the lentils and cook in the vegetable stock with the bay leaf for 25 minutes. The lentils will absorb the liquid and become creamy. Remove the bay leaf.

2 Finely chop the shallots and sweat in a frying pan with a little oil, without browning. Add the curry powder and chilli and leave to infuse for 1 minute.

3 Add the lentils and cook for 2 minutes, stirring constantly. Transfer to a bowl with the cashews and blend to a cream using a hand-held blender. Season with salt, oil and chopped parsley.

4 For the broad bean dip: Rinse and drain soaked beans. Brown the sliced onion in a pan with 2 tbsp of oil. After 7-8 minutes, add the beans and 400 ml of water.

5	**6**
5 Cook until the beans fall apart. Add more water to the pan if necessary. Remove from the heat and blend to a cream using a hand-held blender.	**6** Season with salt, oil and lemon juice, mixing until smooth. Add parsley and paprika as a finishing touch.
7 For the chickpea and walnut dip: chop the onion and sweat in a frying pan with oil for 10 minutes until soft. Add the chickpeas and leave to absorb the flavour of the onions for another 6 minutes, season with salt.	**8** Remove from the heat and blend the chickpeas with the walnuts. Season with vinegar and soy sauce. Serve the dips to accompany crostini, crudités or flatbread.

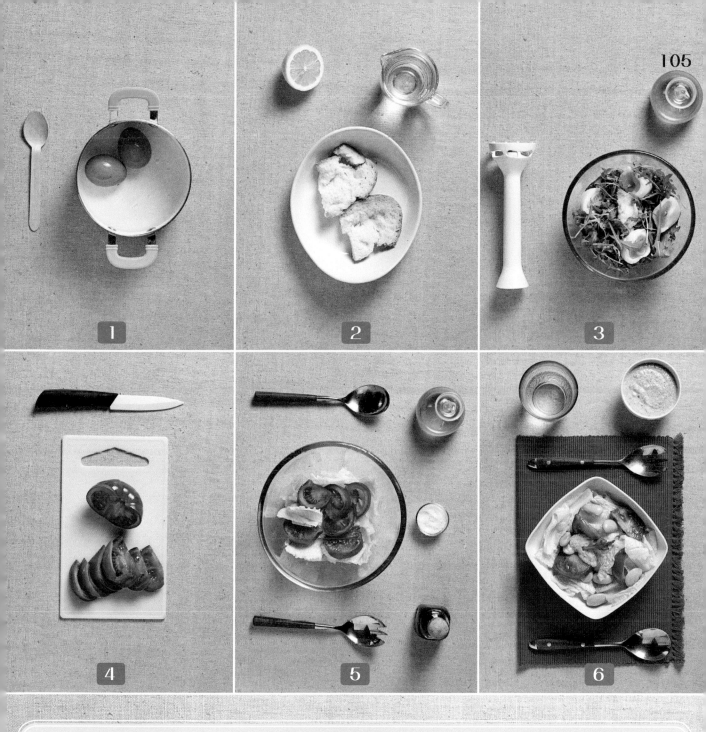

1 Boil the eggs for 5 minutes.	**2** Soften the bread with a little water and lemon juice.	**3** Blend the hard-boiled egg with the rocket and 2 tbsp of oil. Season with salt.
4 Cut the tomatoes into relatively thick slices.	**5** Wash and drain the lettuce, add to the tomatoes and season with salt, oil and vinegar.	**6** Add the beans and dress the salad with the rocket pesto.

CREAM OF BROAD BEANS WITH STIR-FRIED VEGETABLES

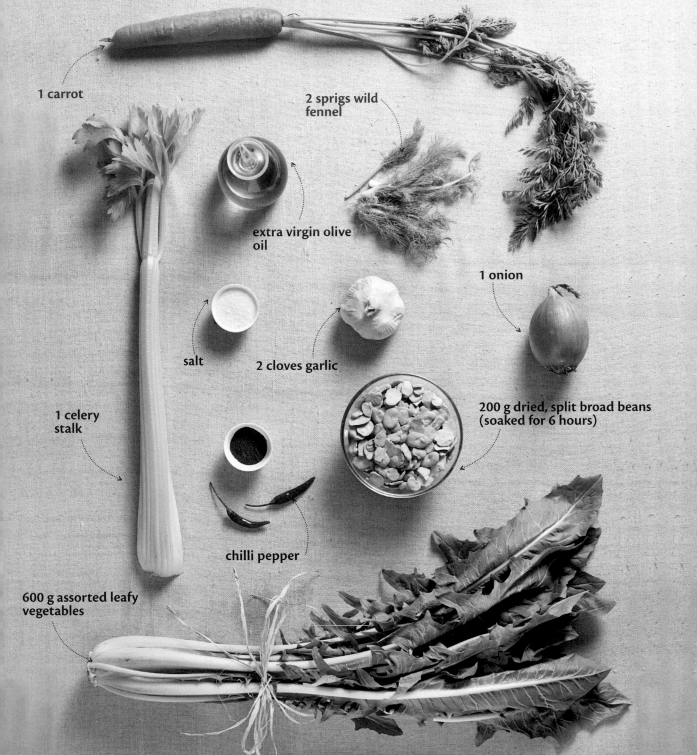

1 carrot

2 sprigs wild fennel

extra virgin olive oil

1 onion

salt

2 cloves garlic

1 celery stalk

200 g dried, split broad beans (soaked for 6 hours)

chilli pepper

600 g assorted leafy vegetables

1. Cook the carrot, onion, celery, fennel and soaked beans in 600-700 ml of water for 1 hour.

2. When the beans have fallen apart, remove from the heat, discard fennel and celery, and blend with oil and salt.

3. Wash the leafy vegetables, removing the toughest parts (central ribs, base of leaves, etc.).

4. Blanch the vegetables for a few minutes in boiling water with a little salt. Set aside some cooking water.

5. Brown garlic and chilli in a wok. Add the vegetables and stir-fry for 10 minutes.

6. Moisten with the saved cooking water. Serve the cream with the vegetables.

MUNG BEAN AND WHEAT SALAD WITH CAPER PESTO

2 pinches oregano

30 g salted capers

250 g cherry tomatoes

1 clove garlic

salt

50 g basil leaves

250 g whole wheat grains

1 teaspoon vinegar

250 g mung beans, cooked

4 tablespoons extra virgin olive oil

2 small courgettes

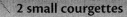

50 g blanched almonds

1

1 Soak the wheat in 500 ml water for 8 hours, then cook in its soaking water.

2 Rinse the salt thoroughly from the capers and combine them with the almonds, basil and oil in a bowl. Blend to a cream using a hand-held blender.

3-4 Slice the courgettes into half-moons. Quarter the tomatoes.

According to Chinese medicine, wheat has cooling properties, making it suitable for summer dishes. It has a calming effect, so it is ideal for restless people, especially children.

5	Sauté the courgettes in a non-stick frying pan with a little oil and the sliced garlic. Season with salt and vinegar.	6	Place the tomatoes in a salad bowl and season with extra virgin olive oil and oregano.
7	Add the cooked mung beans to the courgettes in the frying pan.	8	Add the wheat and mix well. Serve accompanied by the caper pesto.

CREAMY PEA AND LETTUCE SOUP

pepper

4 tablespoons yoghurt

1 litre vegetable stock

salt

1 tablespoon chives

1 spring onion

250 g shelled peas

1 large potato

extra virgin olive oil

1 tablespoon fresh cream

1 head lettuce

1. Peel the potato and cut into pieces. Slice the spring onion and sweat in 1 tbsp of oil.

2. Add the peas after 5 minutes. Add the potato pieces after 3 more minutes.

3. Add the shredded lettuce leaves after another 2 minutes. Then add the stock.

4. Cook for 25 minutes, then blend to a cream using a hand-held blender.

5. Mix the cream with the yoghurt, a pinch of salt and pepper, and the chives.

6. Serve the soup with 1 tbsp of cream.

CHICKPEA, FARRO AND PUMPKIN SOUP

salt

1 slice pumpkin

100 g chickpeas

1 sprig rosemary

1 onion

extra virgin
olive oil

1 bay leaf

250 g farro

2 sage leaves

½ celery stalk

1 Soak the farro in 500 ml of water and the chickpeas in 200 ml of water overnight.	**2** Peel, de-seed and dice the pumpkin.	**3** Chop the onion and brown in a little oil in a heavy-bottomed saucepan.
4 Add the diced pumpkin, chopped celery and herbs to the onion and cook for 5 minutes.	**5** Add the rinsed and drained chickpeas and farro together with its soaking water. Season with salt.	**6** Cover and cook for 2 hours, top up with water if necessary. Remove herbs and season with oil.

BLACK-EYED BEAN SOUP

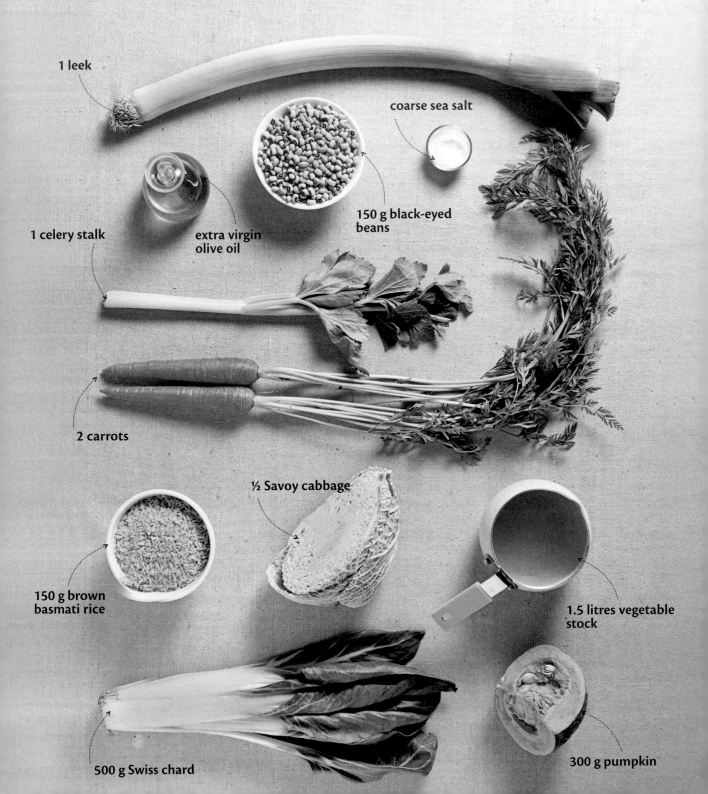

1 leek

coarse sea salt

150 g black-eyed beans

1 celery stalk

extra virgin olive oil

2 carrots

½ Savoy cabbage

150 g brown basmati rice

1.5 litres vegetable stock

500 g Swiss chard

300 g pumpkin

1   Peel and slice the leek. Chop the celery and carrots.

2   Wash the chard and cut it into relatively large pieces.

3-4   Slice the cabbage. Peel the pumpkin and cut into pieces.

Black-eyed beans are the seeds of green beans (*Vigna sinensis* or *Dolichos lablab*) once they are ripe. They were already being eaten before the arrival of bean varieties from the Americas.

5   Combine the sliced leek and chopped celery and carrots in a saucepan with 2 tbsp of oil. Sauté for 3 minutes.

6   Add the beans (previously soaked for 8 hours) and the other vegetables. Mix well, allowing them to absorb the flavours.

7   Add the stock and cook on a high heat for 30 minutes.

8   Add the rice and continue to cook for another 20–25 minutes. Season with salt. Remove from the heat and drizzle generously with extra virgin olive oil.

MALTAGLIATI PASTA WITH FRESH BORLOTTI BEANS

320 g whole grain farro or spelt flour

1 tin whole peeled plum tomatoes

300 g fresh borlotti beans

salt

1 clove garlic

1 celery stalk

2 sage leaves

extra virgin olive oil

¼ onion

1 carrot

1 Work the flour with 1 tbsp of oil and enough warm water to form a relatively soft dough.

2 Wrap the dough in cling film and leave to rest.

3 Dice the carrots, slice the celery and finely chop the onion.

4 Put them in a pan with 1 tbsp of oil, the garlic and the sage and fry.

5 Add the beans and the diced tomato. Cover and simmer for 40 minutes. Season with salt.

6 Roll out the dough 2 mm thick, cut into irregular shapes. Cook and add into sauce.

POTATO AND FARRO GNOCCHI WITH BROAD BEAN PESTO

600 g boiled potatoes

2 tablespoons grated hard vegetarian cheese

350 g fresh broad beans, podded

60 g whole grain farro or spelt flour + 60 g milled farro or spelt flour

1 handful basil leaves

salt

extra virgin olive oil

1 tablespoon grated vegetarian cheese

1 tablespoon pine nuts

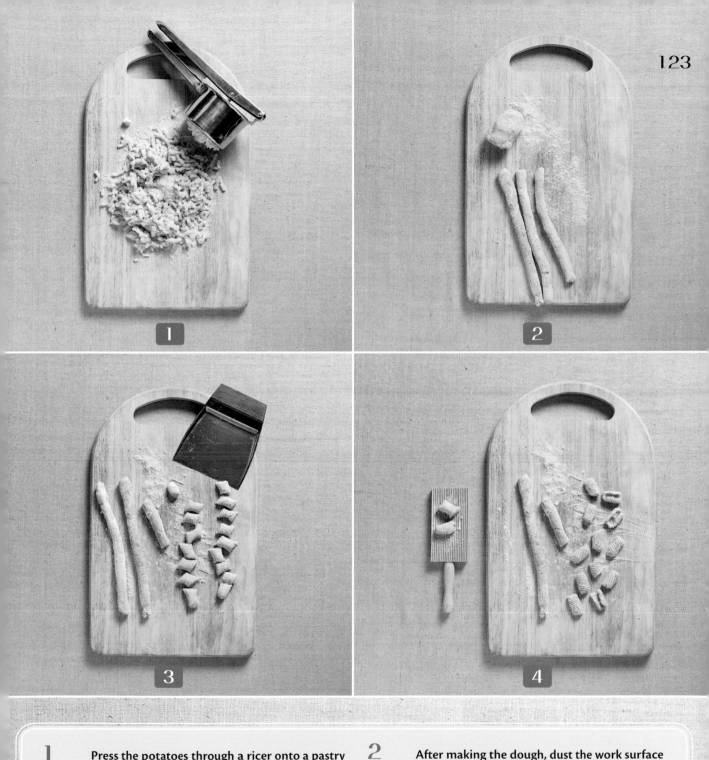

1. Press the potatoes through a ricer onto a pastry board. Sprinkle the work surface with the flour while working until the mixture becomes firm enough to knead.

2. After making the dough, dust the work surface with flour and shape the pasta into 1 cm diameter strings.

3. Form gnocchi by cutting the strings into 2-3 cm long pieces.

4. Give the gnocchi their characteristic ridges using a gnocchi board or by pressing with a fork.

5	**5** Parboil the beans for 3 minutes in lightly salted boiling water.
6	**6** Blend in a liquidiser with the basil, pine nuts and the 2 tbsp of grated hard cheese. Add the oil at the end.
7	**7** Bring the water to the boil, add the gnocchi and cook for 1 minute after they float to the surface.
8	**8** Lift them out with a skimmer and add the pesto. Sprinkle with remaining 1 tbsp grated cheese and drizzle with oil.

POLENTA WITH CAVOLO NERO AND LENTIL SAUCE

2 pinches chilli powder

750 ml water

1 onion

1 tablespoon tomato purée

400 g chopped tomatoes

1 shallot

250 g fine cornmeal

1 clove garlic

1 carrot

250 g lentils

extra virgin olive oil

coarse sea salt

½ celery stalk

10 cavolo nero leaves

1 Finely chop the onion, carrot and celery and sweat in a heavy-bottomed saucepan (even better in an earthenware pot) with the oil.

2 Add the lentils after 5 minutes and fry lightly for several minutes.

3 Add the tomato purée diluted with a little water and the chilli.

4 After 5 minutes, add the chopped tomatoes and bring to the boil. Season with salt, cover the pan and continue to cook over a low heat for at least 1 hour.

5 Clean the leaves of the cavolo nero, removing the central rib, and chop finely.

6 Meanwhile, brown the shallot in another heavy-bottomed saucepan with 1 tbsp of oil until light golden.

7 Add the cavolo nero and cook for 5 minutes. Season with salt, add the water and bring to a boil.

8 Sprinkle in the cornmeal so as not to form lumps. Cover and cook over a very low heat for 15 minutes. Serve the polenta with the sauce and a drizzle of oil.

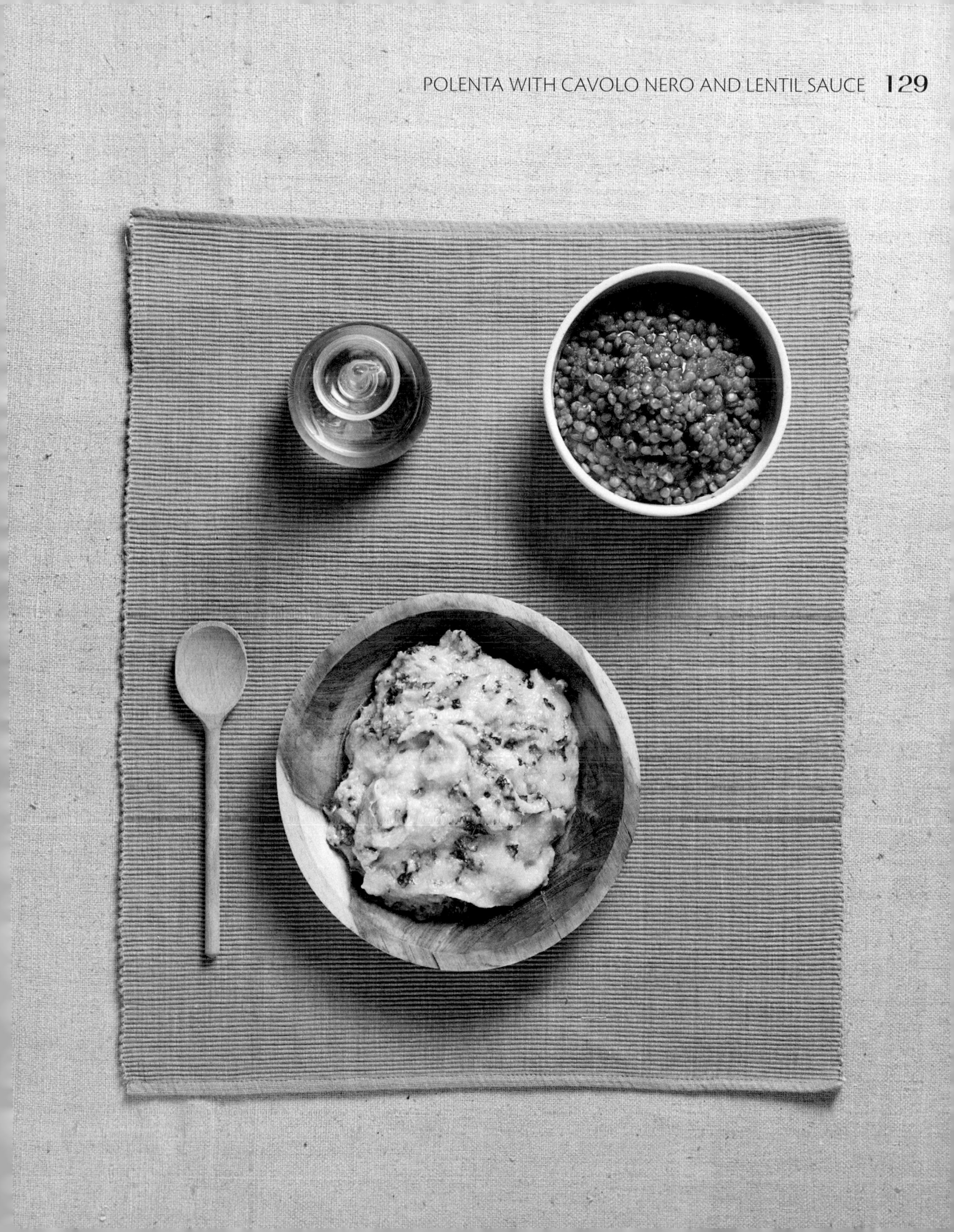

ITALIAN FLATBREAD WITH BEANS, SPRING ONIONS AND PEPPERS

2 spring onions

300 g whole grain farro or spelt flour

1 tablespoon tomato purée

300 g cooked borlotti beans

salt

1 red pepper
1 yellow pepper

1 clove garlic

1 pinch bicarbonate of soda

2 pinches chilli powder

extra virgin olive oil

1 Mix the flour with a pinch of salt and the bicarbonate of soda. Make a well in the flour and place 2 tbsp of oil and 125 ml of lukewarm water inside the well.	**2** Work the ingredients, adding more water if necessary, and knead to a soft, smooth and elastic dough. Wrap in cling film and leave to rest.
3 Meanwhile, clean the peppers and cut into thin strips.	**4** Peel the spring onions and also cut into thin strips.

5. Brown the vegetables with 2 tbsp of oil and the clove of garlic. Season with salt when soft.

6. Add the tomato purée diluted with a little water, cover and cook for 10 minutes. Add the beans.

7. Add the chilli and allow to infuse for 5 minutes.

8. Dust the work surface with flour and roll out the dough to a thickness of 2-3 mm.

9. Heat a non-stick frying pan and cook the flatbreads for 3-4 minutes per side.

10. Fill with the pepper and bean mixture and serve hot.

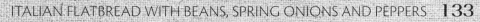

SUMMER VEGETABLE AND CHICKPEA FLOUR MINIBURGERS

200 ml water

1 red pepper

1 red onion

1 courgette

150 g chickpea flour

salt

½ teaspoon oregano

1 pinch turmeric

1 small aubergine

extra virgin olive oil

1	Mix the chickpea flour with the water in a bowl to make a very thick batter. Leave to stand for at least 3 hours.	**2**	Clean the aubergine, courgette and pepper and cut into 0.5 x 3 cm batons.
3	Brown the chopped onion in a little oil. Season with salt and oregano.	**4**	Add the vegetables after 5 minutes and fry lightly for 3-4 minutes.

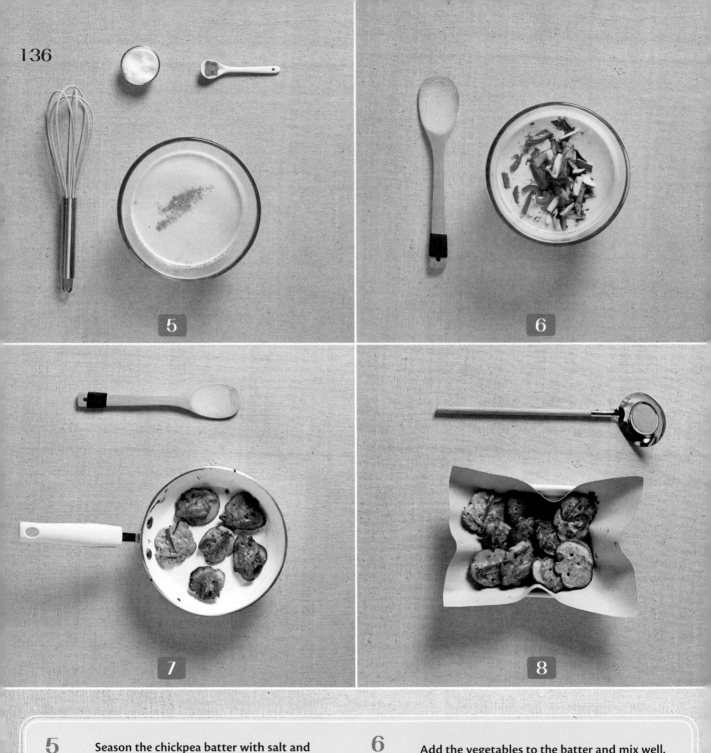

5   Season the chickpea batter with salt and turmeric.

6   Add the vegetables to the batter and mix well.

7-8   Use a spoon to form rissoles. Cook in a frying pan with a little oil until golden. Drain on paper towel and serve hot or cold.

The miniburgers can be accompanied by rice or bulgur wheat, and make a great lunch to take to work.

1 Blend the cooked beans to a cream using a hand-held blender.	**2** Finely chop the carrot, peeled pumpkin and cabbage leaf.
3-4 Lightly fry the chopped vegetables with the garlic and 1 tbsp of extra virgin olive oil. Season with 1 tbsp of soy sauce.	What can be more appetising than rissoles and croquettes? Children always love them. Puréed vegetables can replace eggs as a binder.

5   Combine the bean cream, fried vegetables and chopped parsley in a bowl. Season with salt if necessary.

6   Add a small amount of breadcrumbs to give firmness to the bean and vegetable mixture.

7   Use your hands to shape rissoles and coat them in breadcrumbs, which can be flavoured with rosemary leaves.

8   Heat the oil in a frying pan. Cook rissoles until they are an even golden colour (or cook in the oven at 180°C for about 20 minutes). Serve with soy or sweet and sour sauce.

ADZUKI BEAN, PUMPKIN AND LEEK STEW

1 sprig sage + 2 sprigs thyme
+ 1 sprig rosemary
+ 2 bay leaves

¼ pumpkin

250 g adzuki beans

1 tablespoon soy sauce

extra virgin olive oil

1 leek

coarse sea salt

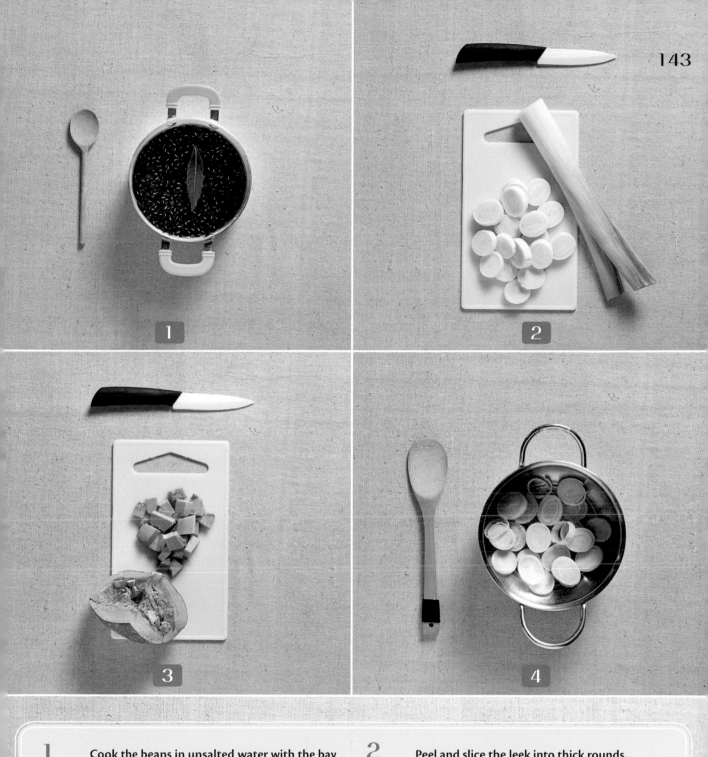

1	Cook the beans in unsalted water with the bay leaves.	**2**	Peel and slice the leek into thick rounds.
3-4	Dice the pumpkin evenly. Heat 2 tbsp of oil in a saucepan and brown the leek for a few minutes.		In Chinese medicine, adzuki beans are very useful for purging toxins from the body; like all pulses, they have an important diuretic effect. They should be included in any low-calorie diet.

5	Add the diced pumpkin to the leek in the saucepan.	**6**	Add each of the herbs one at a time to infuse with their flavours. Season with salt.
7	Add the soy sauce to the vegetables and cook for a few minutes.	**8**	Add the drained adzuki beans with a little of their cooking water. Cover and cook until the pumpkin is tender.

seitan

tempeh

tofu

tofu, seitan & co

From China and Japan, these are essential protein-rich foods for any balanced vegetarian diet.

THE PROTEIN-RICH foods described here are all part of East Asian culinary traditions, particularly those of China and Japan. They have been widely available in Western countries for many years, first as a niche product or simply as an exotic gastronomic curiosity, but now as important complements for a vegetarian diet. It is a fact that our diet contains too much animal protein in relation to our actual requirements (according to present health guidelines, a woman weighing 60 kg needs about 43 g of protein per day), and this puts a serious strain on our organs, particularly the liver and kidneys. Moreover, excess animal protein has an acidifying effect on our body, and this often correlates with osteoporosis, different inflammatory disorders, excess weight and cardiovascular problems. And if that were not enough, this excess consumption also leads to an increased economic burden owing to increased healthcare costs. The use of these sources of plant protein can be a pleasant and light way to vary a diet that is generally high in calories.

A record one in eight British adults has now turned vegetarian according to the latest research from analysts Mintel. Some 12% now follow vegetarian or vegan diets – rising to 20% of those aged between 16 and 24. This ever-increasing interest is due to both ethical and health-related reasons.

TOFU, SEITAN & CO

tofu

Soya milk curdled with magnesium chloride (or other plant-based coagulants) makes tofu, a cheese-like bean curd that is cholesterol-free and an ideal base ingredient for making mayonnaise and other delicious sauces. It can also be deep-fried or pan-fried with flavourings and spices, or used to make creamy desserts. It has the appearance of a soft but compact white or ivory block. It is commercially available as plain tofu or flavoured with herbs or spices. It is easy to digest and a good source of protein and calcium. This makes it suitable for people looking to reduce their animal protein intake. If tofu is eaten with whole grain cereals, it increases the amount of protein that the body is able to use. Chinese medicine considers it to have cooling, diuretic and purgative properties.

To make tofu

500 g soya beans + soaking water, 4 litres of water, 1 cup lemon juice or 1 teaspoon magnesium chloride diluted in 1 cup water

Wash the soya beans and soak for 24 hours, changing the water at least twice. Rinse and blend to a cream with an equal volume of water. Heat 4 litres of water in a pot, add the soya cream and bring to the boil while mixing constantly. When the liquid foams up, add a little cold water and continue to cook on a low heat for 3-4 minutes. Transfer the mixture to a colander lined with a fine-mesh cloth and squeeze out as much water as possible. Return it to the heat and raise the temperature to 90°C. Turn off the heat and add the lemon juice or magnesium chloride to curdle the mixture. Leave to stand so that the curds will separate from the liquid. Strain the tofu by wrapping it in a fine cloth and pressing down on it with a weight. It will keep for 1 week in the refrigerator immersed in water. The remaining soya pulp, known as okara, can be cooked again for 20 minutes and used to enhance the dough used to make crackers and breadsticks, added to stews, or in vegetable pies and tasty croquettes.

SEITAN WITH ARTICHOKES AND FRESH BROAD BEANS

Pour a little oil in a large frying pan and lightly fry 2 thinly sliced shallots for 3 minutes, Then add 320 g of sliced seitan and brown. After 5 minutes, add 2 cleaned and thinly sliced baby artichokes and cook for another 6-7 minutes. Finish by adding 300 g of boiled fresh broad beans and continue to cook for another 3 minutes. Serve the seitan hot or slightly warm with a drizzle of oil.

To make seitan

1 kg white (wheat) flour + 150 g another type of flour, approx. 500 ml hot water for kneading, 2 litres water for the 1st cooking step + 1 tablespoon coarse sea salt, 1 litre water for the 2nd cooking step, 3 tablespoons soy sauce, 1 small onion, 1 carrot, 1 x 5 cm length kombu seaweed, 1 clove garlic, 4 slices fresh ginger, 1 bay leaf, 2 cloves

Place the flour in a large bowl, add the hot water and work the ingredients to make a dough. Transfer the dough to a pastry board and knead until smooth and elastic, adding more flour if it sticks to the work surface. Return the dough to the bowl and cover with hot water. Leave to rest for 30 minutes.
Place the bowl in the sink, discard the water and wash the dough. Fill the bowl with more hot water. Knead the dough under the water; this will turn the dough the colour of milk as the starch is released. Drain off the water and continue to wash and knead, alternating between hot and cold water, until the starch is completely removed. The result will be a ball of elastic gluten. Finish by rinsing in cold water in order to stabilise the gluten strands.
Bring 2 litres of water to the boil with added salt. Cut the seitan in pieces using a knife and cook until it floats, which should take between 5 and 10 minutes. Strain the seitan while waiting for the stock to be ready for the second cooking step.
Combine the aromatics, vegetables, seaweed, soy sauce and spices with 1 litre of water in a saucepan. Cover and boil for 15 minutes. Add the seitan, cover and cook for 30-60 minutes depending on the size of the pieces. Leave the seitan to cool in the stock. When it is cold, it will be ready for use. It will also keep for 4-5 days in the refrigerator, covered in broth inside an airtight container.

seitan

A rich source of plant protein, seitan is made from wheat flour that is made into dough and washed continuously to remove all traces of starch. This creates a slightly gummy substance that consists of little more than gluten. It is then cooked with soy sauce, ginger and kombu to make it ready for use in making other dishes. It is commercially available shrink-wrapped and refrigerated, in jars and as a long-life product. If accompanied by vegetables, seitan makes a protein-rich and completely meat-free meal. It is a very flavoursome and lends itself to highly appetising dishes. It can be fried or grilled with flavourings and spices, or can be the main ingredient for tasty vegetarian sauces.

tempeh

This is obtained from cooked soya beans that are fermented at close to 30°C with a starter culture. It has the appearance of a crusty yellow loaf and a pleasant taste similar to that of chicken. It is high in protein, minerals (calcium and iron), vitamins (B1 and B6), unsaturated fats and lecithin. It is easy to digest and its nutrients are easily assimilated by the body. Fermenting the soya beans increases the biological value of its protein content. It is therefore protein-rich, nutritious, low-fat, easily digested and cholesterol-free food. It is used sliced and fried, sautéed with vegetables, grilled and baked.

HERB TOFUNAISE

2 tablespoons chopped mixed herbs

700 ml water

½ tablespoon de-salted capers

extra virgin olive oil

500 g tofu

4 pickled gherkins

4 tablespoons vegetarian pesto

½ tablespoon miso paste

white vinegar

3 tablespoons soy sauce

½ tablespoon capers in vinegar

salt

pepper

200 g fine cornmeal

2 tablespoons pitted black olives

2 teaspoons mustard

1 lemon

1 pinch curry powder

1 bunch rocket

1 cooked beetroot

1 tablespoon pitted green olives

150

1	Sprinkle the cornmeal into 700 ml of salted water. Cook on very low heat for 15 minutes, stirring constantly.	**2** Remove from the heat. Add the pesto to the polenta and mix well.	**3** Transfer the polenta to a heat-resistant dish and spread out in a 2 cm thick layer.
4	Cut the tofu into pieces and boil in water with 4 tbsp of vinegar. Strain.	**5** Season 4 pieces of tofu with lemon, 5 tbsp of oil, the capers, sliced gherkins and soy sauce.	**6** Blend to a thick, smooth cream using a hand-held blender.

| 7 | | 8 | | 9 | |
| 10 | | 11 | | 12 | |

7 Divide blended tofu into 4 parts: add olives, rocket, 2 tsp vinegar and salt to 1 part.

8 Add the chopped herbs to the second part and season with salt if necessary.

9 Add the curry powder to the third part and mix well.

10 To the fouth part add the mustard, diced beetroot, 1 tbsp of vinegar, salt and pepper, then blend.

11 Crush the remaining tofu with a fork and add the miso paste. Finely chop olives and capers.

12 Mix them with the tofu and add 1 tbsp of oil. Cut the polenta into slices and serve.

SPICY TOFU, MISO, CARROT AND PEPPER SOUP

1 tablespoon extra virgin olive oil

1 tablespoon cornflour

500 ml vegetable stock

150 g tofu in 1 cm dice

1 green pepper

1 tablespoon miso paste

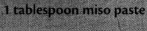

2 spring onions

1 small piece ginger

2 carrots

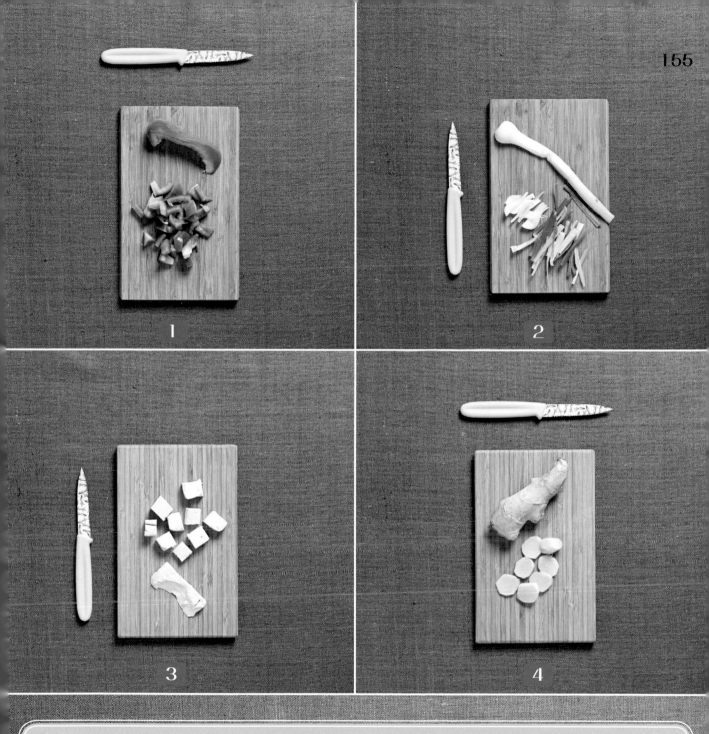

1   Clean the peppers and cut into thin strips.

2   Peel the spring onions and cut into thin strips.

3-4   Chop the carrot into small pieces and dice the tofu. Slice the peeled ginger into 4-5 rounds.

 Chinese meals traditionally start with a soup, which serves to aid digestion.

5 Heat oil in a saucepan and lightly fry the vegetables and ginger.

6 Add the tofu and allow to infuse. Add the vegetable stock and cook over a medium heat for 8 minutes.

7 Dissolve the cornflour in a little water and add to the soup. Continue to cook for 2 minutes, stirring constantly.

8 Dissolve the miso paste in a little water and add to the soup. Serve the steaming hot soup in small bowls.

BASMATI RICE WITH TURMERIC AND PAN-FRIED TOFU

300 g tofu

2 bunches salad leaves

1 handful sunflower seeds

3-4 shallots

320 g basmati rice

balsamic vinegar

extra virgin olive oil

1 teaspoon turmeric

salt

2 pinches chilli powder

1 small head red radicchio

1 small head white radicchio or lettuce

2 tablespoons soy sauce

1 sprig rosemary + 3 sage leaves

2 cloves garlic

1	Slice the tofu, garlic and shallots and place on a plate.	2	Finely chop the rosemary and sage leaves using a mezzaluna knife.
3-4	Season the tofu with the herbs, chilli powder and soy sauce. Cook the rice in salted water infused with turmeric.		Tofu is a truly versatile ingredient. It is irresistible when fried with spices, flavourings and served with different condiments; and it makes a hearty dish when accompanied with a whole grain cereal.

5 Meanwhile, trim, wash and drain the radicchio and salad leaves, tearing the largest leaves by hand. Place in a bowl.

6 Season with salt, extra virgin olive oil and balsamic vinegar.

7 Heat 2 tbsp of oil in a frying pan and pan-fry the tofu slices with the shallot and garlic.

8 When golden, add the sunflower seeds and toast lightly. Serve the tofu with the rice, accompanied with the salad.

SEITAN GOULASH WITH SPICY POTATOES AND BUTTER BEANS

2 tablespoons tomato purée

125 ml red wine

1 bunch herbs (rosemary, sage, bay leaf and marjoram)

salt

½ teaspoon cumin

250 g butter beans, cooked

250 g seitan

2 large potatoes, boiled

extra virgin olive oil

2 large onions

1 fresh chilli pepper

6-7 parsley stalks

2 tablespoons lemon juice

1 tablespoon paprika

1   Peel and finely slice the onions.

2   Sweat over a low heat with 2 tbsp of extra virgin olive oil.

3-4   Cut the seitan into 3-4 cm pieces and add. Season with salt and pepper and brown over a high heat. Add the wine and reduce completely. Sprinkle in the paprika and cook.

This is a vegetarian version of an iconic central European dish. Depending on how it is cooked, seitan has a similar flavour and texture to meat.

5 Add the tomato purée diluted with a little water.	**6** Add the herbs, cover and cook for 30 minutes. Add water if necessary.	**7** Peel the cooked potatoes and cut into pieces.
8 Finely chop the chilli pepper, parsley, cumin and 1 clove garlic (optional).	**9** Combine the potato pieces and beans in a bowl.	**10** Season with the chopped aromatics, lemon juice and salt. Serve with the goulash.

SEITAN, CARROT, POTATO AND PEA MEDALLIONS

1 spring onion

1 bunch
mixed salad leaves

2 carrots

extra virgin olive oil

½ lemon

1 handful fine cornmeal

200 g seitan

200 g peas

salt

1 bay leaf

2 large potatoes,
boiled and
crushed

1 bunch
baby radicchio

5-6 radishes

1 bunch rocket

1	Chop the spring onion and seitan, and brown with 1 tbsp of oil and bay leaf.	2	Add the diced carrot and peas. Remove the bay leaf and season with salt. Cook for a few minutes.	3	Transfer to a bowl and incorporate the crushed potatoes.
4	Shape the mixture into medallions and dredge in the cornmeal. Transfer to a greased baking tray.	5	Add the radishes to the salad leaves. Dress with oil and 2 tbsp of lemon juice and salt.	6	Drizzle the medallions with oil and cook in the oven at 200°C for 10 minutes.

SEITAN WITH FRIED FRENCH BEANS AND CHERRY TOMATOES

300 g cherry tomatoes

2 pinches oregano

balsamic vinegar

320 g seitan

salt

2 sage leaves

1 tablespoon ginger juice

300 g French (green) beans

extra virgin olive oil

2 sprigs thyme

1 sprig rosemary

1 tablespoon lemon juice

2 handfuls breadcrumbs

1 clove garlic

2 tablespoons soy sauce

1   Slice the seitan, lay the slices on a plate
     and brush lightly with oil.

2   Finely chop the herbs and mix with the
     breadcrumbs.

3-4   Dredge the seitan slices in this mixture. Boil
      the beans until they are tender but still very
      firm. Drain and cut into 3-4 cm lengths.

Seitan, when accompanied by French beans, makes a
well-balanced dish because of its protein content. It
is also light and flavourful, and suitable for working
people who are unable to have meals at home.

5 Heat 2 tbsp of oil in a wok with the crushed garlic and lightly fry the beans until they are very shiny. Remove from the heat and season with salt and balsamic vinegar.

6 Quarter the tomatoes. Transfer to a bowl and season with salt, oregano and oil.

7 Prepare the vinaigrette with the soy sauce, lemon juice, ginger juice and 1 tbsp of oil.

8 Fry the seitan with 2 tbsp of oil until golden, then serve with the vinaigrette and vegetables.

POTATOES STUFFED WITH 'CHILLI CON SEITAN'

250 ml tomato
passata (sauce)

50 g sweetcorn

4 large potatoes

1 onion

salt

½ tablespoon
Mexican spice blend

300 g romaine (or
iceberg) lettuce

200 g kidney beans

extra virgin olive oil

balsamic vinegar

200 g seitan

½ carrot

1   Peel the carrot and onion. Finely chop together with the seitan.

2   Place the chopped ingredients in a saucepan with 1 tbsp of oil and brown for 5 minutes.

3-4   Season with the spice blend. Add the tomato passata and beans. Season with salt, cover and cook over a low heat for 25 minutes.

This is a delicious vegan version of an iconic Tex-Mex dish, and is also an ideal meal for people who want to take a packed lunch to work.

5   Meanwhile, wash the potatoes well, cut in half lengthwise and steam for 10 minutes.

6   Use a melon baller to hollow out the potatoes, leaving a 5 mm thick layer of flesh on the skin.

7   Fill the potatoes with the 'chilli con seitan'. Arrange on an oiled baking tray and cook in the oven at 200°C for 10 minutes or until the potatoes are cooked through.

8   Break up the lettuce leaves, add the sweetcorn and dress with oil and vinegar. When the potatoes come out of the oven, leave to cool a little, then serve with the salad.

TOFU AND TEMPEH SKEWERS WITH BROCCOLI AND CHERRY TOMATOES

1 tablespoon
ginger juice

1 head broccoli

¼ teaspoon + 2 pinches
chilli powder

1 tablespoon
sesame oil

200 g tempeh

soy sauce

1 clove + 2 slices
garlic

200 g tofu

extra virgin olive oil

balsamic vinegar

2 pinches cumin

salt

300 g cherry tomatoes

1 pinch oregano

1 bunch mixed herbs
(marjoram, chives,
basil)

1 Cut the tofu and tempeh into 1.5 cm cubes.	**2** Mix the sesame oil with 1 tbsp of vinegar, 2 tbsp of soy sauce, 1 slice of garlic (chopped), the chilli powder, oregano and cumin.
3 Add the tofu and tempeh and marinate for at least 30 minutes.	**4** Wash the broccoli, cut into florets and blanch in boiling water for 3 minutes.

5	Place the crushed garlic clove in a frying pan with 2 tbsp of oil and cook for 1 minute.	6	Add the blanched broccoli and sauté over a high heat for 3 minutes, stirring constantly.	7	Prepare the skewers and grill or cook in the oven at 240°C, basting with the marinade.
8	Wash and cut up the cherry tomatoes on a chopping board.	9	Chop the herbs and place in a bowl with the garlic, season with oil, salt, vinegar and ginger juice.	10	Add the tomatoes and mix well. Serve the skewers with the vegetables.

FRIED TEMPEH WITH LEEK TAGLIATELLE AND HAZELNUTS

4 leeks

2 tablespoons soy sauce

1 tablespoon lemon juice

1 tablespoon ginger juice

1.5 litres vegetable stock

1 tablespoon chopped onion

150 g toasted hazelnuts

½ teaspoon turmeric

nutmeg

320 g tempeh

½ tablespoon rice flour

½ teaspoon thyme leaves

1   Whisk the soy sauce in a cup with
    1 tbsp of oil, the ginger juice, lemon juice
    and thyme.

2   Brush the sliced tempeh with this emulsion
    and leave to infuse.

3   Trim the leeks, cut them lengthwise and wash
    well. Cut the centre into 3-4 mm wide strips.

4   Blanch for 30 seconds and shock in an ice bath
    to keep them crisp.

5   Use a heavy-bottomed saucepan to heat 1 tbsp of olive oil and sweat the onion with the turmeric.

6   After 5 minutes, add the flour and toast well while stirring. Add the vegetable stock and bring to the boil, thickening the sauce.

7   Away from the heat, add nutmeg and the hazelnuts. Season with salt and blend.

8   Fry the tempeh in a frying pan with 1 tbsp of oil. Serve accompanied by the leek tagliatelle dressed with the hazelnut sauce.

sesame seeds

sunflower seeds

cashew nuts

black sesame seeds

pumpkin seeds

Brazil nuts

flax seeds
(linseed)

macadamia nuts

pine nuts

walnuts

hazelnuts

nuts & seeds

Rich in nutritional properties, these
have been used for centuries to
produce oil, or to eat raw but
there are still many uses for them
in cooking.

almonds

pistachio nuts

NUTS & SEEDS

NUTS AND SEEDS stand out for their high fat content; in fact, they have been used for centuries to extract oils for food use. The fats they contain are mainly high quality unsaturated fats that are easily digested. Nuts and seeds are also high in protein, dietary fibre and essential minerals, among which are potassium, magnesium, phosphorous and iron, and vitamins B, D, E and A.

In order to benefit fully from their nutritional properties, they should be chewed thoroughly. Nuts and seeds should also be eaten recently harvested because their essential oils turn rancid. Owing to the significant presence of oil, they are often very useful for stimulating gastrointestinal transit. Chinese medicine considers them an excellent source of energy. In fact, like all seeds (including pulses and cereals), they have the potential to bring forth a new plant and therefore provide their own life-giving energy. Given this large energy potential, they should be eaten as a course on their own or as a high-energy snack, not as an extra at the end of a meal. Nuts and seeds lend themselves to countless uses in cooking: as an ingredient for an invigorating muesli at breakfast and salads; as a delicious accompaniment for starters where they add crunch; and also as an ingredient to enhance gratins and desserts.

They are extremely versatile, not only plain or lightly toasted, but also blended into creams for preparing different kinds of appetising sweet and savoury sauces.

hazelnuts

Hazelnut trees were widespread in Europe, even before cultivation began of olives and grapes. They contain vitamins A, B1, B3 and C, and are high in minerals, especially calcium, phosphorous and magnesium. They have a high content in easily digested fat and a mild laxative effect. According to Chinese medicine, in addition to their digestive effects, they are an effective remedy against intestinal parasites, particularly tapeworm. Lightly toasted hazelnuts are ideal for making cakes and pastries. They can also be puréed and combined with honey and cocoa to make an exquisite spread. Hazelnuts are used to make nougat and brittles, and are a perfect ingredient for dishes featuring raw or cooked vegetables and whole grains.

almonds

Almonds originated in the Middle East and are perfectly acclimatised to the Mediterranean region of Europe. Sweet almonds contain a large amount of magnesium and are high in calcium and phosphorous. They also have plenty of dietary fibre, potassium and zinc. They therefore have great food value, and have always been the perfect accompaniment for vegetarian and raw food diets. They are actually a stimulant and rebalance the nervous system. According to Chinese medicine, they stimulate lung function, soothe coughs and are a mild laxative. Peeled and chopped almonds soaked in water produces a refreshing, thirst-quenching and energy-giving drink. Almonds can be used to make countless desserts and are a basic ingredient in fruit and cereal breakfast preparations, in addition to brittles and nougats, cakes and pastries. Toasted and lightly salted almonds are an ideal accompaniment for salads and cooked vegetables.

pistachio nuts

Pistachios are indigenous to the eastern Mediterranean. They have a high protein content, and contain iron, calcium, phosphorous, magnesium and potassium. They have restorative and stimulating properties for the nervous system and for treating anaemia. Pistachios were used in the past as a purgative and for treating liver problems. Chinese medicine considers them as a Yang or energy food, and prescribes them for lower back pain and impotence. They are used in cooking to flavour all kinds of desserts, gelato in particular.

pine nuts

These sweet, aromatic and slightly resinous seeds are high in protein. They are an ideal source of minerals owing to their high phosphorous and potassium content. They are a restorative suitable for pregnant women, elderly people, people with anaemia and for treating constipation. In cooking they are a basic ingredient for making pesto and strudel filling. They are an excellent complement for all sorts of sweet and savoury dishes.

walnuts

The walnut tree is a native of Central Asia that was brought to Europe in ancient times. Walnuts contain a large amount of oil and are a good source of minerals owing to their content in phosphorous, magnesium and potassium, with small amounts of iron and calcium. They are considered in naturopathy as a stimulant for the nervous system, useful in cases of asthenia and intense intellectual work. They have antiseptic and digestive properties. Chinese medicine uses walnuts to treat asthma and constipation, particularly in older people. An excellent energy drink is made by blending 5-6 kernels with 2 ripe pears and 2 teaspoons of honey. Walnuts have a very pleasant and slightly piquant flavour. They are very delicate nuts which need to be stored in a cool and dry place to prevent them from turning rancid. Walnuts are used in a large number of dishes and preparations: cream cheese, desserts with honey, pie fillings, pasta sauces and salads with vegetables and fruits.

Pecan nuts. These nuts are the American cousins of the European walnut. They have a rich and sweet flavour but they are very high in calories.

Brazil nuts. These nut are characterised by their hard, triangular shell and soft, white flesh. They tend to turn rancid very easily, so you should buy only freshly harvested nuts in their shells. Their very high fat content means that they are particularly rich in magnesium and zinc. They are recommended for people who are underweight or suffering from anaemia or fatigue.

coconut

The dried pulp of the coconut is very high in saturated fat. For this reason, it should be used sparingly. However, it contains a great deal of dietary fibre (for instance, it is used to treat eating disorders).

Chinese medicine considers it a good remedy against intestinal parasites. In cooking, coconut is mainly used in a dessicated and dried form in sweet preparations, while Oriental cuisines use it to vitalise countless sweet and savoury dishes.

cashew nuts

The cashew tree is native to the Amazon basin. Cashew nuts are always toasted before they reach us because they contain a slightly toxic oil that breaks down with heat. It is a good source of minerals owing to its content in iron and phosphorous, and it is also a source of vitamins B1 and A. It is a very common ingredient in Indian cuisine and common in typical nut mixes found in Britain and the United States.

flax seeds

These seeds have long been used for their laxative and soothing properties. Chinese medicine makes use of them to treat skin problems, particularly dermatitis. One traditional use was to make hot poultices which were placed on the chest as a remedy for coughs caused by colds. They are added to bread, and also ground up and used in soups, mixed with vegetables and in muesli.

sunflower seeds

These seeds pack a healthy punch, as they are full of protein and linoleic acid, rich in vitamins B1 and D, and contain important amounts of iron and magnesium. As a result, they are truly 'wonder seeds', with properties that protect the digestive system from cancers and strengthen the immune system. They combat anaemia, high blood pressure and high cholesterol. They are good for the skin and nails, the eyes and the heart. They are used in bread, salads and dishes made with cereals. They also make an ideal snack.

pumpkin seeds

These seeds were highly prized fifty years ago, and have recently made a comeback owing to their interesting properties. They are high in vitamins B and E, and contain good amounts of the essential fatty acids omega 3 and omega 6, in addition to iron and dietary fibre. They are effective against intestinal worms, and are recommended for children suffering from these 'invasions'. They also have an anti-inflammatory effect on the prostate and urinary tract. They add a special touch to salads, and are an essential ingredient of roasted mixed seed snacks, and are an excellent addition to any dish.

sesame seeds

Native to India, sesame seeds contain a great deal of dietary fibre and are high in magnesium, calcium, phosphorous, silicon, iron and B-group vitamins. They are alkaline and energy-giving, and have restorative properties for the muscles and nerves. They are used in Chinese medicine to treat dry coughs, constipation and anaemia. They are used, typically lightly toasted, to enrich cereal and vegetable dishes, or to flavour bread and breadsticks, and are the basic ingredient for sesame snaps. As a cream, known as tahini, they are used to make pulse sauces, such as hummus.

SPICY SEED AND NUT MIXES WITH GRAPEFRUIT MOCKTAIL

½ tablespoon cane sugar

100 g blanched almonds

400 g pink grapefruit juice

3 pinches chilli powder

4-5 tablespoons soy sauce

100 g cashew nuts

2 cardamom pods

4 tablespoons ginger juice

3 pinches sweet paprika

salt

150 ml water

3 pinches hot curry powder

100 g unsalted peanuts, shelled

100 g Brazil nuts

1 Place 1 tbsp of soy sauce in each of 4 small bowls. Mix the curry powder in the first bowl, with paprika in the second, with chilli powder in the third, and 1 tbsp of ginger juice in the fourth.

2 Roast the almonds in the oven at 180°C until they turn a deep golden colour.

3-4 Add them still hot to the bowl with the ginger juice and coat them well with the liquid. Add the peanuts to the bowl with the chilli.

It's time to stop the high-calorie foods that make snack time a health hazard. Here is a recipe that allows you to surprise your guests with a tasty snack, without giving them a nasty surprise on the bathroom scales.

5   Add the previously roasted Brazil nuts and the almonds to the bowl with the hot curry powder.

6   Add the cashews to the bowl with the paprika. As they are already toasted, hazelnuts and cashews only need heating in a frying pan before use.

7   Bring water to the boil with the sugar and split cardamom pods. Leave to cool, then strain into a jug.

8   Add the grapefruit and ginger juices and a pinch of salt. Mix and serve the mocktail with ice to accompany the spicy seed and nut mixes.

MULTI-SEED CRACKERS

100 g fine cornmeal

½ teaspoon coarse sea salt

3 tablespoons extra virgin olive oil

200 g organic whole grain wheat flour

1 tablespoon poppy seeds

1 teaspoon black sesame seeds

2 teaspoons dry yeast

1 tablespoon mustard seeds

1	Lightly toast the seeds in a frying pan, then leave to cool.	2	Combine the two flours with the salt, yeast and seeds on a pastry board and make a well.	3	Place the oil and some lukewarm water in the well to form a firm and elastic dough.
4	Knead the dough, then rest for 30 minutes. Divide the dough into different pieces.	5	Roll the pieces out into thin sheets and cut out crackers with a pastry wheel.	6	Transfer to a baking tray and bake at 180°C for 10 minutes.

RADICCHIO, CHEESE AND WALNUT TARTE TATIN

250 g Italian '00' flour

5 tablespoons white wine

1 tablespoon poppy seeds

½ tablespoon honey

100 g butter

80 g hard vegetarian cheese

pepper

350 g radicchio

extra virgin olive oil

coarse sea salt

½ tablespoon white sesame seeds

½ tablespoon black sesame seeds

6 walnut kernels

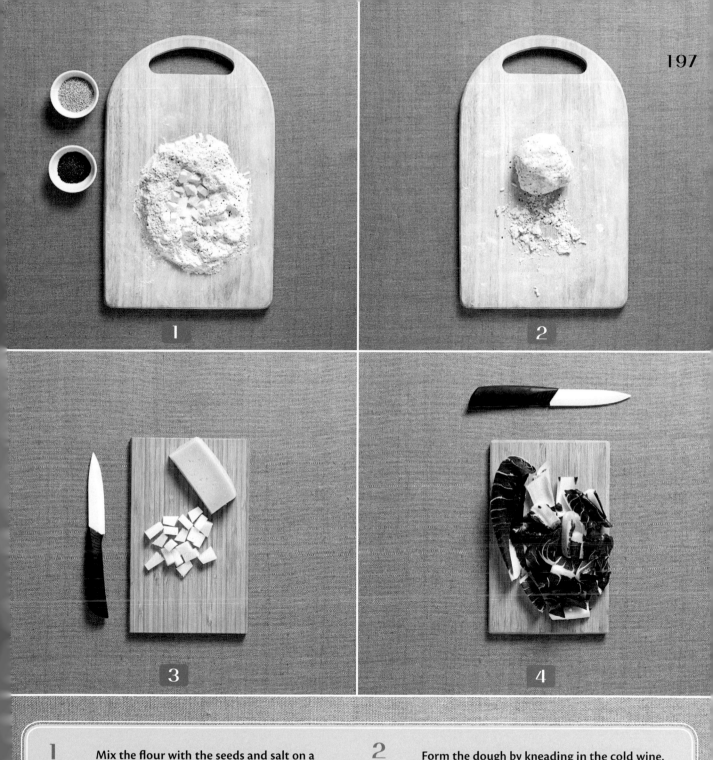

1 Mix the flour with the seeds and salt on a pastry board. Add very cold butter in pieces and incorporate into the flour.

2 Form the dough by kneading in the cold wine. Wrap in cling film and leave to rest for at least 30 minutes.

3-4 Cut the cheese into dice. Wash and drain the radicchio leaves and cut into 3-4 cm pieces.

To add more flavour to the radicchio, it can be wilted in a frying pan with 1 tbsp of balsamic vinegar.

5	Cook radicchio in a frying pan with 1 tbsp of oil and a pinch of salt.	6	After 3 minutes, add the honey and caramelise. Remove from the heat.	7	When cool, add the cheese and a pinch of pepper.
8	Grease two 10-12 cm diameter moulds and fill with the walnuts.	9	Add the cooked radicchio.	10	Roll out the pastry 4-5 cm thick and cover the contents of the moulds. Bake at 180°C for 30 minutes.

YELLOW TAGLIATELLE WITH ONION, BABY SPINACH AND MIXED SEEDS AND NUTS

120 g Italian '0' flour

extra virgin olive oil

100 g whole grain flour

1 sachet ground saffron

2 tablespoons pistachio nuts, shelled

125 ml white wine

300 g baby spinach

coarse sea salt

100 g durum wheat flour

1 large red onion

1 tablespoon sesame seeds

2 tablespoons pine nuts

1   Mix the flours on a pastry board and make a well in the centre. Place 1 tbsp of oil and the saffron dissolved in a little water in the well.

2   Work in the wine and knead into a smooth and elastic dough. Cover in cling film and leave to rest for about 30 minutes.

3   Thinly slice the onion and sweat gently in 1 tbsp of oil. Season with salt.

4   Add the spinach and continue to cook for no longer than 2 minutes.

5   Gently toast the pine nuts, sesame seeds and pistachios in a frying pan.

6   Roll the dough out into a thin sheet. Make the tagliatelle by rolling the sheet and cutting strips with a knife (or using a pasta machine).

7   Cook in boiling salted water for 5-6 minutes. Drain and sauté quickly with the vegetables, adding a little cooking water.

8   Sprinkle the toasted seeds and nuts over the saffron tagliatelle and serve.

TRICOLOUR TERRINE WITH CRISPY CRUST

1 handful sunflower seeds

1 sprig rosemary

1 sage leaf

300 g pumpkin

coarse sea salt

parsley

1 handful breadcrumbs

1 clove + 1 slice garlic

300 g spinach or chard

300 g potato

extra virgin olive oil

2 pinches nutmeg

1 spring onion

1 Dice the pumpkin and cook until soft with a little oil, the garlic clove, sage and rosemary. Add a little water while cooking.

2 Cook the potato for about 30 minutes in boiling water, then peel. Press through a potato ricer.

3 Drizzle with oil and season with salt and a little grated nutmeg.

4 Finely chop the spring onion and sweat in a frying pan with 1 tbsp of oil. Add the chopped greens, season with salt and cook until tender.

5		6		7	
5	Chop the breadcrumbs with the parsley, slice of garlic, sunflower seeds and salt.	**6**	Transfer to a bowl and mix with a little oil.	**7**	Grease a dish, sprinkle with breadcrumbs and put in a layer of mashed potato.
8	Make a second layer with the greens.	**9**	Remove the herbs and garlic from the pumpkin and mash. Finish with a layer of mashed pumpkin.	**10**	Sprinkle with chopped sunflower seeds and bake at 200°C for 10 minutes or until brown.

PEAR, ALMOND AND GINGER CREAM WITH AMARETTI BISCUITS

4 very ripe pears

1 tablespoon almond cream

2 tablespoons chopped hazelnuts

4 amaretti biscuits

2 tablespoons dark chocolate chips

1 tablespoon ginger juice

1 vanilla pod

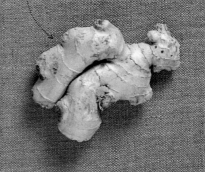

1 Peel the pears and cut into pieces on a chopping board.	**2** Cook with the vanilla pod. When the pears are soft, remove the vanilla (it can be reused if washed and dried).
3 Extract the juice from a piece of peeled ginger by squeezing the grated pulp. Add to the cooked pears.	**4** Mix well and add the almond cream.

| 5 | Blend to a cream using a hand-held blender. | 6 | Place 1 amaretti biscuit at the bottom of 3 small bowls or ramekins. |

| 7-8 | Pour the pear, ginger and almond cream over them. Before serving, sprinkle the top with chocolate chips and chopped hazelnuts. | | This is not only a delicious dessert, but according to Chinese medicine, it is perfect for protecting the respiratory system from attack during the cold season. |

APRICOT AND PISTACHIO SWEETS
WITH APPLE TEA

50 g unsalted pistachios
+ 10 g for decorating

1 teaspoon black tea

200 g dried apricots

1 apple

40 g cane sugar

1 vanilla pod

1	Chop the dried apricots and pistachios separately.	**2**	Mix together and form little fruit and nut balls.
3-4	Roll the balls in the cane sugar. Decorate each one by pressing ½ a pistachio into the top.		Organic dried fruit cannot be treated with sulphur dioxide so it will always have a brown colouring, the sign of natural processing without chemical residues.

214

| 5 | Cut the apple into thin slices. | 6 | Boil the apple slices with the vanilla pod for 10 minutes. |

| 7 | Strain the liquid and pour into a cafetière. Add the black tea. | 8 | Add a cup of cold water. Leave to infuse and serve with the sweets. |

FRESH FRUIT, HAZELNUT AND ALMOND CRUMBLE

50 g flaked almonds

1 pear

1 banana

1 apple

1 tablespoon extra virgin olive oil

salt

raspberries

1 tablespoon ginger juice

50 g coarsely chopped hazelnuts

2 tablespoons cane sugar

120 g rolled oats

blueberries

strawberries

2 tablespoons lemon juice

1   Peel the apple, pear and banana, and cut into pieces. Wash and quarter the strawberries.

2   Add the lemon and ginger juices and 1 tbsp of sugar to the fruit.

3-4   Mix the rolled oats with the extra virgin olive oil in a bowl. Add the cane sugar to the oats.

Crumbles are typical Northern European sweet preparations that are ideal for breakfast or as a nourishing sweet snack.

5   Add the flaked almonds and chopped hazelnuts.

6   Mix thoroughly with 1-2 tbsp of water and a pinch of salt.

7   Place the fruit in lightly greased ramekins or individual baking dishes.

8   Cover with the oat crumble and nuts. Bake in the oven at 200°C for 15 minutes. Serve warm.

CEREAL BRITTLE

2 tablespoons coarsely chopped hazelnuts

70 g puffed rice

2 tablespoons corn oil

70 g puffed barley

100 g rice or corn malt syrup

4 tablespoons raisins

70 g puffed quinoa

2 tablespoons flaked almonds

1	Heat the malt syrup with the corn oil in a wide saucepan until it turns liquid.	**2** Add the puffed cereals, raisins, almonds and hazelnuts. Mix well.
3	Spread the mixture out in a 1.5 cm thick layer in a greased baking dish. To make a denser brittle, cover with baking parchment and compact with a steak hammer.	**4** Bake in the oven at 180°C for 15 minutes. When cool, break up the brittle with your hands or use a knife to cut bars.

INDEX

LEGEND:

⊘ MILK FREE   ⊘ EGG FREE   ⊛ GLUTEN FREE   ⊘ VEGAN

PULSES

Creamy bean dips 94

Courgette and bean paté sandwiches 98

Pulse dips 100

Garden salad and rocket pesto 104

Cream of broad beans with stir-fried vegetables 106

Mung bean and wheat salad with caper pesto 108

Creamy pea and lettuce soup 112

Chickpea, farro and pumpkin soup 114

Black-eyed bean soup 116

Maltagliati pasta with fresh
borlotti beans 120

Potato and farro gnocchi with broad bean pesto 122

Polenta with cavolo nero and lentil sauce 126

Italian flatbread with beans, spring onions
and peppers 130

Summer vegetable and chickpea flour
miniburgers 134

Cannellini bean and vegetable rissoles 138

Adzuki bean, pumpkin and leek stew 142

TOFU, SEITAN & CO.

Herb tofunaise 150

Spicy tofu, miso, carrot and pepper soup 154

Basmati rice with turmeric and pan-fried tofu 158

Seitan goulash with spicy potatoes
and butter beans 162

Seitan, carrot, potato and pea
medallions 166

Seitan with fried french beans
and cherry tomatoes 168

Potatoes stuffed with 'chilli con seitan' 172

Tofu and tempeh skewers with broccoli
and cherry tomatoes 176

Fried tempeh with leek tagliatelle
and hazelnuts 180

NUTS & SEEDS

Spicy seed and nut mixes with
grapefruit mocktail 190

Multi-seed crackers 194

Radicchio, cheese and walnut
tarte tatin 196

Yellow tagliatelle with onion, baby
spinach and mixed seeds and nuts 200

Tricolour terrine with crispy crust 204

Pear, almond and ginger cream with
amaretti biscuits 208

Apricot and pistachio sweets with
apple tea 212

Fresh fruit, hazelnut and almond
crumble 216

Cereal brittle 220

Other books of interest published by Grub Street available from all good bookshops, or from www.grubstreet.co.uk or from other online retailers

Classic Vegetarian Cookery
Arto der Haroutunian
978-1-908117-01-4

Divine Vegan Desserts
Lisa Fabry
978-1-908-117-29-8

The Green's Cookbook
Extraordinary Vegetarian Cuisine
Deborah Madison
978-1-906502-58-4

Sprouts and Sprouting
Valerie Cupillard
978-1-904943-90-7

Raw Cakes
Caroline Fibaek
978-1-909808-16-4

Raw Snacks
Caroline Fibaek
978-1-909-808-05-8

Vegetarian Dishes from the Middle East
Arto der Haroutunian
978-1-902304-81-6

Verdura
Vegetables Italian Style
Viana La Place
978-1-906502-78-2

Vegetable Heaven
Sensational Seasonal Vegetarian Recipes
Catherine Mason
978-1-904943-53-2

Veggie Burgers Every Which Way
Lukas Volger
978-1-908117-19-9

Vegan with a Vengeance
Isa Chandra Moskowitz
978-1-904943-66-2

Vitally Vegetarian
Tina Scheftelowitz & Christine Bille Nielsen
978-1-910690-04-8